Heliostat Manufacturing for Near-Term Markets: Phase II Final Report

National Renewable Energy Laboratory (NREL)

The BiblioGov Project is an effort to expand awareness of the public documents and records of the U.S. Government via print publications. In broadening the public understanding of government and its work, an enlightened democracy can grow and prosper. Ranging from historic Congressional Bills to the most recent Budget of the United States Government, the BiblioGov Project spans a wealth of government information. These works are now made available through an environmentally friendly, print-on-demand basis, using only what is necessary to meet the required demands of an interested public. We invite you to learn of the records of the U.S. Government, heightening the knowledge and debate that can lead from such publications.

Included are the following Collections:

Budget of The United States Government
Presidential Documents
United States Code
Education Reports from ERIC
GAO Reports
History of Bills
House Rules and Manual
Public and Private Laws

Code of Federal Regulations
Congressional Documents
Economic Indicators
Federal Register
Government Manuals
House Journal
Privacy act Issuances
Statutes at Large

September 1998 • NREL/SR-550-25837

Heliostat Manufacturing for Near-Term Markets

Phase II Final Report

Energy Products Division
Science Applications International Corporation
Golden, Colorado

National Renewable Energy Laboratory
1617 Cole Boulevard
Golden, Colorado 80401-3393
A national laboratory of the U.S. Department of Energy
Managed by Midwest Research Institute
for the U.S. Department of Energy
under contract No. DE-AC36-83CH10093

NREL/SR-550-25837

Heliostat Manufacturing for Near-Term Markets

Phase II Final Report

Energy Products Division
Science Applications International Corporation
Golden, Colorado

NREL technical monitor: Al Lewandowski

National Renewable Energy Laboratory
1617 Cole Boulevard
Golden, Colorado 80401-3393
A national laboratory of the U.S. Department of Energy
Managed by Midwest Research Institute
for the U.S. Department of Energy
under contract No. DE-AC36-83CH10093

Prepared under Subcontract No. ZAP-5-14178-02

September 1998

NOTICE

This report was prepared as an account of work sponsored by an agency of the United States government. Neither the United States government nor any agency thereof, nor any of their employees, makes any warranty, express or implied, or assumes any legal liability or responsibility for the accuracy, completeness, or usefulness of any information, apparatus, product, or process disclosed, or represents that its use would not infringe privately owned rights. Reference herein to any specific commercial product, process, or service by trade name, trademark, manufacturer, or otherwise does not necessarily constitute or imply its endorsement, recommendation, or favoring by the United States government or any agency thereof. The views and opinions of authors expressed herein do not necessarily state or reflect those of the United States government or any agency thereof.

TABLE OF CONTENTS

LIST OF FIGURES

LIST OF TABLES

1.0 INTRODUCTION

The Solar Manufacturing Technology (SolMaT) program is an initiative of the U.S. Department of Energy's Concentrating Solar Electric Program. Objectives of the SolMaT program are to:

Develop manufacturing technology that permits deployment of solar thermal power systems in low-volume, early commercial applications;

- Reduce uncertainty in the cost and reliability of key solar components;

- Promote development of system-level business plans and industrial partnerships linking manufacturing scenario to commercial sales prospects; and,

- Establish a manufacturing base for achieving substantial cost reductions through high volume production of solar thermal components.

The project described in this report is cost-share funded by the U.S. Department of Energy through the National Renewable Energy Laboratory (NREL) for the development of heliostats for central receiver power systems. In this project, Science Applications International Corporation (SAIC) and its subcontractors Boeing/Rocketdyne and Bechtel Corp. are developing manufacturing technology for production of SAIC stretched membrane heliostats. The result of this project will be to better position SAIC to manufacture and sell these heliostats for markets between now and early part of next decade.

The project consists of three phases, of which the first two have now been completed. This first phase had as its goals to identify and complete a detailed evaluation of manufacturing technology, process changes, and design enhancements to be pursued for near-term heliostat markets. In the second phase, the design of the SAIC stretched membrane heliostat was refined, manufacturing tooling for mirror facet and structural component fabrication have been implemented, and four proof-of-concept/test heliostats have been produced and installed in three locations. The proposed plan for Phase III calls for improvements in production tooling to enhance product quality and prepare for increased production capacity.

1

2.0 SUMMARY OF PHASE II RESULTS

SolMaT Phase II has been successful in attaining the main goals of the project, which were to fabricate key pieces of semi-automated tooling for heliostat production, demonstrate the tooling with a production of four heliostats, and install/test the heliostats. The semi-automated tooling developed and fabricated by SAIC for facet production was shown to be very successful in reducing the labor content in the facets by a factor of 70%. Improvements were also made in the areas of quality and repeatability of the finished product. SAIC has now produced about 170 facets with this tooling at a rate of 2 facets per day with a crew of 2 to 3 people. Boeing/Rocketdyne was successful in demonstrating semi-automated torque tube and truss tooling developed for this project.

Incremental improvements were made in the heliostat design as compared to the design package produced in Phase I of the project. Although a few changes were made in facet design, the majority of the changes were in the heliostat structure. The original 18" diameter torque tube was found to be insufficiently stiff and was replaced with a 24" torque tube to provide the required stiffness. Additional structural analysis on the heliostat was done to verify the design. A photograph of the Phase II stretched membrane heliostat is shown in **Figure 2-1**. SAIC refined the design of the control system developed in Phase I and fabricated four systems plus spares for testing in Phase II. Improvements were made to increase the functionality and reliability of the control system during the test program.

Tooling concepts that were developed in Phase I were refined in Phase II with detailed design drawings produced for each tool. A major effort went into the design and fabrication of the membrane tensioner/ring weld tool, which is the major tooling accomplishment of Phase II. Although fabrication of this tool was the most expensive effort under Phase II, this tool has allowed the greatest reduction in labor content for heliostat facets. Other tooling fabricated include upgrades to the membrane welding process, vacuum platens for membrane transfer processes, and mirror lamination equipment. The cost and layout of a 2,000 heliostat per year production facility were updated from the Phase I conceptual design and heliostat production costs were estimated based on the production plant design.

The heliostat production costs at a rate of 2,000 units per year was estimated to be $28,400 per unit, or $157.00 per square meter of mirror. At this level of production, there are 3.2 man hours of labor content per facet.

The four heliostats produced in this program were installed at the NREL Mesa Top Facilities, the Sandia National Solar Thermal Test Facility, and at the Solar Two central receiver power plant in Daggett, California. Optical testing of the heliostat at Sandia by SunLab staff found the reflected image to be comparable to that predicted by CIRCE before fabrication of the heliostats. However, at the relatively short slant ranges for these tests, spreading of the beam into two images caused by off-axis aberration at low incident angles to the heliostat was encountered. The 170 M2 heliostat is probably best suited to larger central receiver systems, and may require a size reduction for small fields.

(Solmat3.to1)

Figure 2-1. Photograph of Phase II Stretched Membrane Heliostat

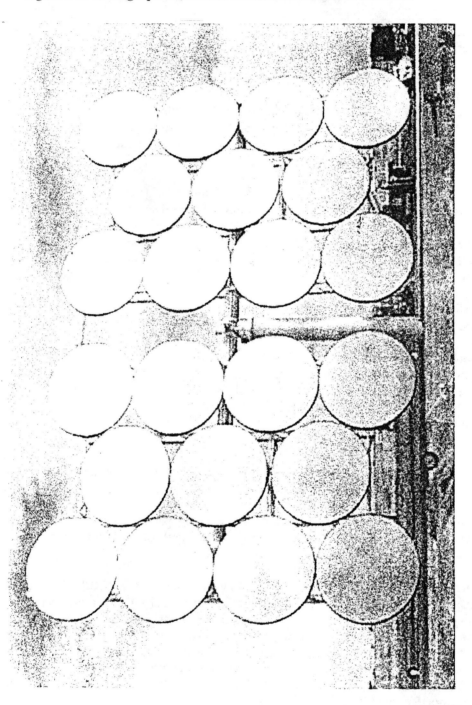

(Solmat3.to1)

An analysis of the market for heliostats was accomplished by Bechtel, which showed the price the heliostats must attain for various market nitches. Their analysis showed that a cost of $120 per meter squared is needed to attain a significant share of the commercial power market. Thus, the present design has not yet attained sufficient cost reduction to meet commercial market demands.

A plan and cost estimate for continuation of the project to Phase III is presented. This plan calls for quality improvements of some of the key pieces of tooling, and development of tooling not addressed in SolMaT to this point. The plan also calls for development of some key components of the heliostat, such as an advanced low-cost drive system. Lessons learned in Phase II of the project are also presented.

(Solmat3.to1)

3.0 HELIOSTAT DESIGN

The SAIC heliostat consists of 22 3.2-m diameter stretched-membrane facets mounted on a torque tube/truss support structure. The total reflective area of the heliostat is 170 m^2. Shown below are design issues addressed in Phase II of the project.

3.1 Facet Design Revision

The facet design was reviewed at the beginning of Phase II. A single-membrane design with mild steel membranes was found unworkable, so the design reverted to a double-membrane, stainless-steel membrane facet. In order to reduce complexity and cost in the production line, an investigation was performed that concluded that the extra cost of stainless steel for the ring would be justified compared with the cost of coating mild steel.

A cost comparison was made between thin (1.0 mm) and thick (3/32", 2.4 mm) glass mirrors for the facets. Although the initial costs of thick glass are less, and it is available in larger sheets, the reflectance is less. The conclusion from the trade-off analysis was that the cost of thin glass would be paid back in 9 years due to increased optical performance of heliostat. Due to the uncertainties in market conditions, the 3/32" glass was selected to reduce the initial cost of the heliostat.

3.2 Optical Analysis

In the Phase II effort, additional analyses were performed to evaluate the effects of facet focusing, wind and gravity-induced focusing of facets, and the effect of canting on the image shape as a function of the time of day. The results of these analyses are summarized in the following subsections.

3.2.1 Analysis of Focused/Unfocused Facets

CIRCE runs were performed to calculate the predicted image size of individual facets as a function of their focus condition and slope errors. **Figure 3-1** shows the results of the analysis for both flat and parabolic facets for conditions similar to the Sandia heliostat/tower. The results are summarized in **Figure 3-2**, which shows the radius containing 90% of the power for focused and flat facets as a function of the surface slope errors of the facets. The conclusion is that the image sizes are significantly different only if the facet slope error is less than 1 mrad, and the image sizes are never larger than a typical receiver. These results support the decision to not focus the heliostat.

3.2.2 Wind-Induced Focusing

A large number of CIRCE runs were performed to try and pin down what we should allow for wind focusing/defocusing of the facets on our heliostat. For reference, our measurements at about 15 mph wind on the dish facets gave a focal length of about 500m, and ranges of receiver distances of interest are 120 m to 450 m for the Solar Two plant, and 250m to 1250m for the APS 100 MW power plant design.

5

Figure 3-1. Flat and Parabolic Facets with Target at 250m

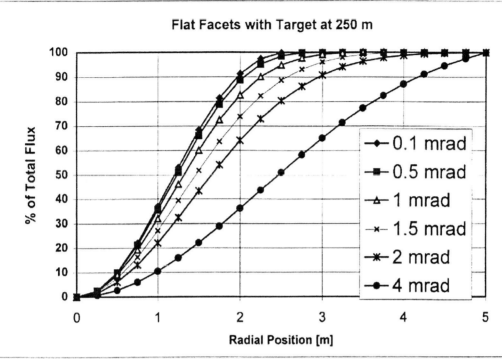

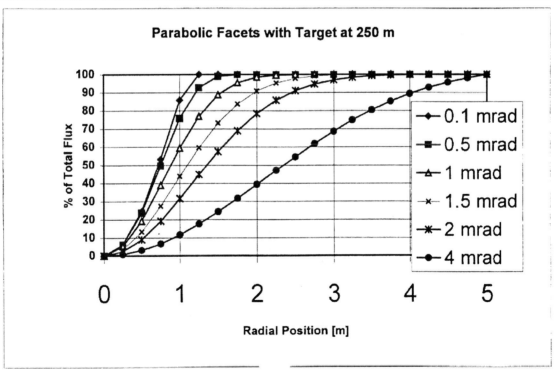

(Solmat3.to1)

Figure 3-2. SolMaT Heliostat Results at 250m Focal Length

Radius at 90% flux:

Error (mrad)	0.1	0.5	1	1.5	2	4
Flat Facets	1.97	2.05	2.25	2.57	2.95	4.17
Parabolic	1.07	1.21	1.55	1.97	2.45	4.05

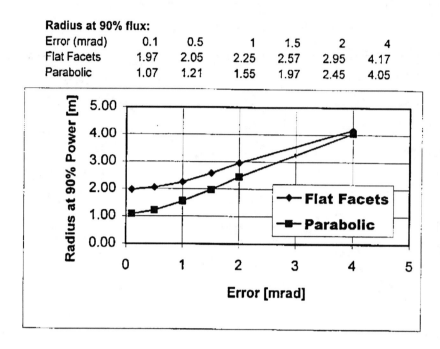

A flat facet was used as a baseline for comparison. **Figure 3-3** shows the amount of power intercepted as a function of receiver radius and distance to the target for this facet. As shown, heliostat facets close to a receiver (e.g., 250 m) deliver 100% of the reflected energy into a circle about 4 m in radius. As the distance increases, so does the radius of the circle, so that at 1,000 m distance, only 57% of the energy gets into a 4 m radius circle.

Comparing a flat facet to a focused facet, to first order one would expect the focused facets to be better over a range of target distances up to about twice the focal length of the facet. The best performance would be expected at the focal distance, with the improvement from a flat facet decreasing away from that point. This is illustrated in **Figure 3-4**. This intuitive understanding was validated by the CIRCE results.

Using the same type of intuitive argument, a facet focused with a negative focal length should produce worse results than a flat facet over the entire range of target distances. The "badness" of the results should be inversely proportional to the focal length. A flat facet is the same as a facet with infinite focal length, so the performance of "defocused" facet approaches that of a flat facet for long focal lengths. The intuitive effect is illustrated in **Figure 3-5.**

7

Figure 3-3. Flat Heliostat Facet

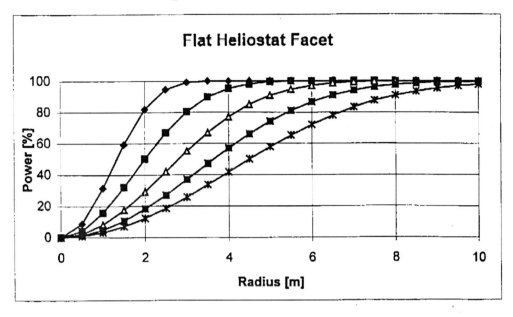

Figure 3-4. Image Size from a Focused Facet vs. a Flat Facet

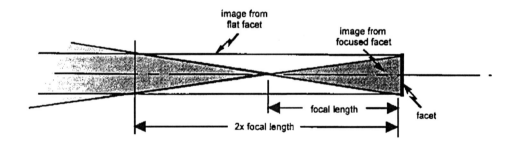

Figure 3-5. Image Size from Defocused Facet vs. a Flat Facet

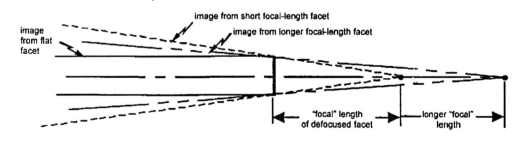

8

Again, this intuitive result was verified in the CIRCE analyses. The result of these considerations is that focused facets are likely to be as good or better than flat facets for focal lengths around 500m and distances to the receiver from 100m to 1,250m. On the other hand, defocused facets are likely to give significantly worse performance than flat facets for these conditions.

The next question is how would these effects show up in a field of heliostats. Since the heliostats point in different directions around the receiver, it is likely that some parts of a field would see rear winds (causing defocusing) at the same time other parts of the field were seeing frontal winds (causing focusing). Also, the effect of gravity is always tending to focus the facets, since they are always pointed upward when operating. These two considerations lead one to believe the effects of wind defocusing will be ameliorated to a great (although unquantified) extent.

To come up with a quantitative basis on which to compare the results, the effort looked first at the radius of the images as a function of focal length and distance to the receiver, as shown in **Figure 3-3** for a flat facet. **Figures 3-6** and **3-7** show the results. The "Representative Radius" shown on the bottom is a radius determined by calculating the first moment (with radius) of the flux profile. It corresponds to something like a 1-standard-deviation radius of the flux profile. The other curve shows the 95% power radius for the various cases. Also plotted on the graphs are the Solar Two and APS 100 MW receiver sizes and distances for the heliostat fields.

Because it was so difficult to come up with a good single radius that represented the flux from a facet, another approach was tried, shown in **Figure 3-8**. In this case, an 8 m diameter receiver was chosen (e.g., for an APS 100 MW plant), and the spillage that would result for various focal lengths and distances was calculated. The results are shown on the first page of the attachment. One of the immediate conclusions from the graph is that focused focal lengths longer than about 500 m are indistinguishable from the flat facet, but shorter focal lengths (250 m) spill significantly more energy outside of about 500-750 m distance. This is as expected from the intuitive analysis presented above.

Since the focused facets don't seem to be a problem, the effort concentrated on the defocused facet results. Shown on the figure are results for defocused facets with focal lengths from -250 m to -2000 m. As shown, the short focal lengths of -250 m and -500 m spill significant amount of energy, whereas the longer focal lengths (-750 m to -2000 m) become almost undistinguished from the flat facet.

Next, a uniform density of heliostats in the field was assumed and a total spillage over an entire field of heliostats was calculated. This helped integrate out the comparative differences, and resulted in the curve shown on **Figure 3-9**. At a focal length of -2000m, the total spillage is only about 20% more than with flat facets. However, the knee in the curve occurs between about 500 m and 1,000 m, and spillage at shorter focal lengths becomes extreme.

(Solmat3.to1)

Figure 3-6. Distance to Target (m) — Radius at 95% Power (m)

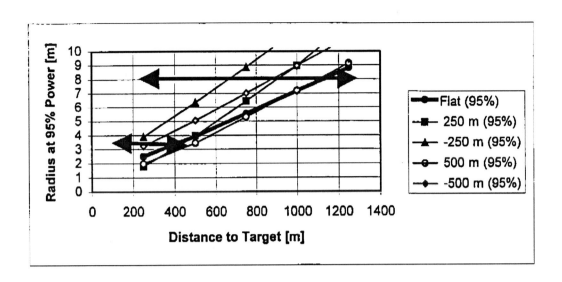

Figure 3-7. Distance to Target (m) — Representative Radius of Image (m)

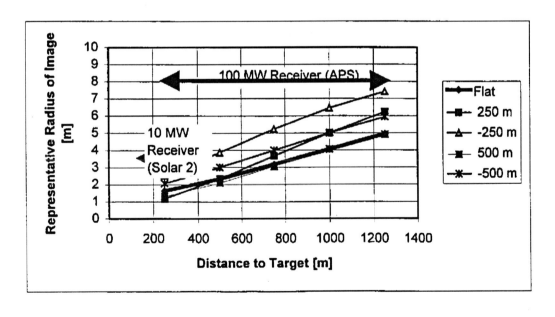

10

Figure 3-8. Spillage With 8m Radius Receiver

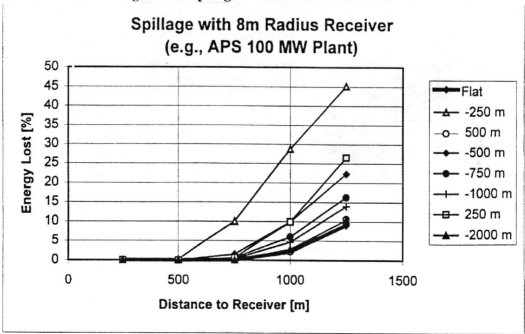

Figure 3-9. Spillage Due to Wind-Induced Focal Length

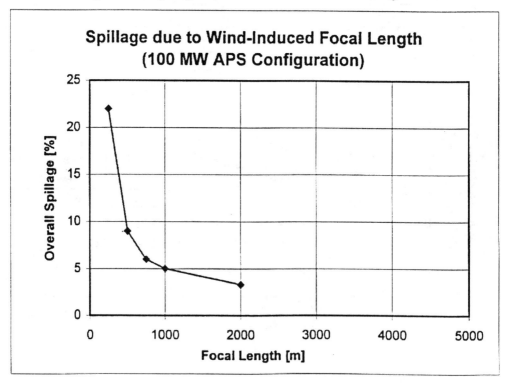

11

From these results, it is difficult to come to a precise conclusion. The effects of the focal length should ideally be analyzed compared to the cost of attaining a particular value. Also, as described above, the effects of wind are various at different locations in a field of heliostats, not to mention that the wind itself becomes non-uniform when introduced into an array of heliostats. So, the best that we can hope for from these analyses are some guidance as to the scale and scope of the effects. Finally, the effects are dependent on the size of the heliostat field considered, and the size of the receiver.

With all of the preceding factors in mind, it seems to be that a tolerance of +/- 500 m focal length at 15 mph wind would not be unreasonable. This value is predicted to lead to 9% spillage for a 100 MW field if all facets were defocused at 500m, but spillage would be practically the same as for flat facets (i.e., 3%) if all facets were focused at 500m. Since it is likely that some facets would be focused and others defocused by the same wind, and since the gravity effect is to focus the facets, the potential effect would probably be somewhere between these values. Thus, perhaps 5% spillage off a 100 MW receiver might occur in a 15 mph wind. This seems to me a reasonable amount. Also, for smaller fields, which are more likely to be implaced in the near future, all of these effects are reduced.

In September 1996, measurements were made of the deflections induced in the membranes of facets at the JVP Phase I dish system due to wind. The result was that the deflection was nearly linear with wind speed, and a 1.4mm. deflection was measured at a wind speed of 15 mph.

3.3   Heliostat Design Criteria

3.3.1   Heliostat Environmental Requirements
The heliostat system is designed to operate within the following environmental limits:

Temperature:
-30°C to +50°C (-22°F to 122°F7)

Relative Humidity
0% to 100%

Altitude/Barometric Pressure:
-400 in to 3000 in (-1300 ft to 9700 ft) elevation

Wind:
The wind reference height is 10 in (32.8 ft). The velocity of the wind is assumed to follow a power law dependence on elevation from the ground, $v = v_{10m}(h/10m)^{15}$. Other assumptions about the wind are as follows:

- Maximum wind rise rate: 0.01 M/S2 (0.02 mph/s)
- Deviation from horizontal: ± 6.6'
- Wind averaged over 5 minutes

(Solmat3.to1)

- Peak gusts 1.6 times average

The requirements on the heliostat are as follows:

- Operate within specifications with average winds up to 7 m/s (15 mph)
- Survive, without damage, peak gusts up to 22 m/s (50 mph) while moving to stow from any orientation
- Survive, without damage, peak gusts up to 40 m/s (90 mph) in the stow position

Rain/Snow:
- The heliostat shall sustain no damage from rain.
- The heliostat shall support a 25 kg/m^2 (5 lb/ft^2) snow load in stow position without damage.
- The heliostat shall support a 50 mm (2 in) ice deposit without damage.

Lightning:
- The heliostat structure shall survive a direct lightning strike without damage.
- The heliostat controls may sustain damage from direct strike, but controls are not to be damaged from a lightning strike to an adjacent heliostat.

Hail:
- The heliostat shall survive 1" hail without damage in the stow position (denting of the rear membrane is allowed).
- Seismic
- The heliostat shall survive +1 g acceleration from any direction in any orientation without damage. It shall survive conditions of seismic zone 3 without damage.

3.3.2 Structural Requirements

Heliostat Structure
Total Operational Structural Optical Error Budget: 0.06° (1 mrad) RMS slope error

Using the geometry of the faceted heliostat (layout #8), and assuming that the slope errors are proportional to the distance of the facets from the center of the heliostat, the allowable errors for each facet in order to give an overall average error of 1.0 mrad are summarized below. The facet group designations are shown in **Figure 3-10**.

Facet Group	Allowable Error	Edge-to-Edge Deflection
a	0.43 mrad	1.3 mm
b	0.85 mrad	2.6 mm
c	0.82 mrad	2.5 mm
d	0.97 mrad	3.0 mm
e	1.32 mrad	4.0 mm
f	1.51 mrad	4.6 mm

13

Figure 3-10. Facet Group Designations

Figure not available

The edge-to-edge deflection is the z-direction deflection allowable across the width (3.05m/10') of a facet resulting from the allowable error. For reference purposes, the following table summarizes some data about the deflections needed for canting a faceted heliostat for different positions in a heliostat field.

Position in Field	Distance	Cant Angle Range	Edge-to-Edge Deflection
100 MW, far-field	1250 m	1.0 to 3.5 mrad	3 to 10 mm
100 MW, near-field	230 m	5.4 to 19 mrad	16 to 58 mm
10 MW, far-field	430 m	2.9 to 10 mrad	8.8 to 31 mm
10 MW, near-field	Horn	11 to 39 mrad	33 to 120 mm

Facet Optical Error
Allowable Facet Optical Error: 0.06° (1 mrad) RMS slope error

Wind-Induced Deflections
Wind-Induced Tracking Deflection at 12 m/s: 0.11° (1.9 mrad) RMS

Tracking Range of Motion
Unrestricted Tracking Range: 180°+ in azimuth
minimum elevation at least -90° (face-down stow)
maximum elevation at least 120° (i.e., 30° "over shoulder")

Heliostat Canting/Focusing
Facet Canting Capability: adjustable from 110 m to 1250 m target slant range
Facet Focus Capability: none

3.3.3 Electrical/Control Requirements

Positioning Precision: 0.06° (1 mrad)
Slew Speed: 0.05 rpm (18°/minute)
(to allow movement to stow of 180° maximum within 10 minutes)
Communication: 14.4+ kbaud serial to central computer
plug-in hard-wired local controller
Heliostat Power Supply: 120 VAC; 50/60 Hz

3.4   Heliostat Structural Analysis

The heliostat design selected for production is shown in **Figure 3-11**. The heliostat is a multi-faceted design with 22 stretched membrane facets. The facets are mounted to flat vertical trusses, which are connected to torque tubes. The torque tubes attach to either side of a central azimuth/elevation drive unit, which surmounts a central pedestal. The multi-faceted heliostat design was chosen after a trade-off study that showed it would be less expensive to produce than the initial baseline design, which was a dual module heliostat.

15

(Solmat3.to1)

Analysis was performed on the SOLMAT heliostat structure to evaluate the effects gravity and wind on the structure. This report will summarize the analyses performed to determine the stress and deflection of the system under these loads. The structural analysis of the heliostat system consists of a loads analysis that produces the loads to be applied to the structure, and a finite element analysis that produces stresses and displacements of the system. The methodology and major assumptions used in these analyses will be discussed.

LOADS ANALYSIS

Wind Load Calculation:

- Wind loads used in the structural design of the concentrator were developed according to the recommendations in "Wind Load Design Methods for Ground Based Heliostats and Parabolic Dish Collectors", By J.A. Peterka and R. G. Derickson, SAND92-7009, September 1992.

Figure 3-11. SAIC Multi-Faceted Stretched Membrane Heliostat

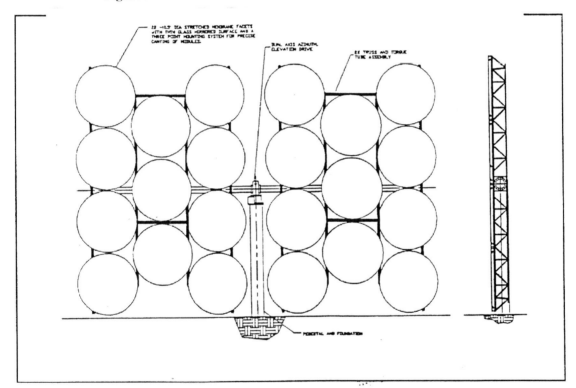

Performance Requirements:

- The concentrator was designed to meet the above performance specification for mean wind speed up to and including 15 MPH. At mean wind speed above 15 MPH, the concentrator will begin to move toward a stow position.

16

- The concentrator was designed to survive a mean wind speed of 31 MPH (gusts to 50 MPH) at any attitude without structural damage.
- The concentrator was designed to survive a mean wind of 56 MPH (gusts to 90 MPH) in the stow position without structural damage.

Load Calculations:
- Loads calculated using relations described in "Wind Load Design Methods for Ground Based Heliostats and Parabolic Dish Collectors" produce a single value for the force and moment on the heliostat at the location of the drive in any orientation. For use in modeling, these loads are distributed across the surface of the heliostat to produce appropriate resultant forces and moments.
- The loads used for analysis of the structure to verify performance were the mean loads caused by the mean wind described above. Mean loads were calculated using the dynamic pressure generated by the mean wind and mean wind load coefficients.
- The loads used for analysis of the structure to verify survival without structural damage were the peak loads caused by gusts during the mean wind described above. Peak loads were calculated using the dynamic pressure generated by the mean wind and peak wind load coefficients.
- The ratio of peak gusts to mean wind was assumed to be 1.6.
- 31 mph mean wind has 50 MPH peak gusts
- 56 mph mean wind has 90 MPH peak gusts

Environmental Assumptions:
- The dish was isolated (no load reduction factors due to blockage).
- The mean and peak wind was defined at a height of 10 m (32.8 ft).
- The power law exponent for mean velocity variation with elevation was that of an open country environment: .17
- Boundary layer wind was assumed to follow the following power law:
  $$U(Z)/U(Zref)=(Z/Zref)^n$$
  where,

$U(Z)$	= mean velocity at height Z
$U(Zref)$	= mean velocity at reference height Zref
n	= power law exponent (a measure of ground roughness)

Geometric Assumptions:
- The porosity of the faceted dish due to open space between facets is considered significant. The area used to determine the force due to wind was 80% of the actual area enclosing the concentrator outline as shown in **Figure 3-12**.

- The chord length used in the calculation of wind load is the length of the side of a rectangle enclosing the concentrator outline as shown in **Figure 3-12**. The rectangle height is used as the chord length for elevation moment calculations. The rectangle width is used as the chord length for azimuth moment calculations.

17

Wind Load Distribution:

- The force and moment generated by wind is distributed across the surface of the heliostat as forces normal to the heliostat surface at the center of the facets. The following methodology is used to develop the force distribution

  ⇒ Force and moment on the heliostat is calculated using wind load relations in Peterka et al.

  ⇒ Force distribution is assumed to be proportional to wind dynamic pressure distribution which is defined as $Q=.00256*[U(z)]^2$ where $U(z)$ is defined above.

  ⇒ Two constants are introduced, one is a slope offset and one is a force offset. These constants are used to generate a set of two equations and two unknowns equating the force and moment calculated using relations in Peterka et al. with the force and moment generated by forces distributed across the surface of the heliostat.

Figure 3-12. Concentrator Outline

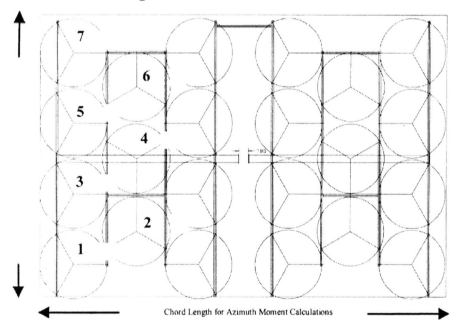

Chord Length for Azimuth Moment Calculations

LOADS RESULTS

For the current effort, it was determined that stresses and displacements would be evaluated at the three critical orientations that are expected to produce the worst loading conditions for the heliostat system;

Orientation   *Wind Speed*

18

(Solmat3.to1)

Elevation 30 Degrees	50 MPH gusts
Elevation 90 Degrees, Azimuth 65 Degrees	50 MPH gusts
Stow	90 MPH gusts

Tables 3-1 and 3-2 (attached) show the calculated forces and moments for these wind speeds. Forces and moments taken from these tables were used to determine forces on each facet for a particular wind speed/orientation combination. This calculation involved determining forces on each facet that would produce the resultant loads calculated in the spreadsheets above. Mathematica was used to perform this calculation. Facet forces are summarized below and the Mathematica programs for the three wind speed/orientation combinations are attached. In the following tables, the facets are numbered 1 to 7. Facet 1 is the top four facets, 2 is the next highest two facets, etc:

Orientation - Alpha 30°, 50 MPH Peak Gusts

Facet Number	Force (lb)
1	1408.8
2	1212.62
3	1003.59
4	778.921
5	535.303
6	247.677
7	-29.8979

Orientation - Stow, 90 MPH Peak

For this case, the lift and drag were combined as the square root of the sum of the squares to determine a resultant force. This force was then assumed to be applied perpendicular to the fact and surface as drag. The Mathematica program was then rum to produce the following facet forces.

Facet Number	Force (lb)
1	1403.32
2	1237.38
3	1237.38
4	841.969
5	593.902
6	259.218
7	-47.09

Orientation - Alpha=90,Beta=65 ROTATED, 50 MPH Peak Gusts

This orientation produces a maximum azimuth moment. The Mathematica program was developed to determine a vertical force distribution to account for elevation moments only. Since this orientation produces critical torque tube loads, it was important to develop a force distribution to evaluate the effect of the loads on the system. In this case, the Mathematica

19

(Solmat3.to1)

program calculated forces on facets in vertical columns rather than horizontal rows. As seen in **Figure 3-12** above, there are 6 columns of facets. Four columns of four facets and two columns of 3 facets. The Mathematica program was modified to calculate forces on these rows of facets, which produce an azimuthal moment when, applied. For this case, the lift and drag forces were linearly combined and applied as drag in the program.

Facet Number	Force (lb)
1	1448.75
2	1321.53
3	1174.0
4	895.961
5	614.942
6	-91.1172

FINITE ELEMENT ANALYSIS

A finite element model of the heliostat system was developed. The model was made using 3 dimensional beam elements. The geometry was modeled to include the structural modifications to stiffen the torque tubes and add diagonal supports. Appropriate material and section properties were applied. For each case, the forces shown above were divided by 3, and applied to the appropriate facet attachment point. The facets were modeled using 3 stiff beam elements in a triangle. The mass density of those elements was determined so that the 3 beam elements weigh the same as a single facet. The facet attachment brackets were modeled using appropriately sized beam elements with all rotational degrees of freedom free at the facet attachment. The drive was not modeled and will add significant flexibility to the system. The location of the drive was assumed to be fixed. Gravity was applied to all models.

RESULTS

Stresses and deflections in the heliostat trusses and torque tubes are shown in the following pages. The following table summarizes the results. The results for gravity-only analyses are also included in the table:

Alpha 30°, 50 MPH Peak Gusts

Max Stress (psi)	19487
Max Displacement (inches)	2.6

Stow, 90 MPH Peak

Max Stress (psi)	19039
Max Displacement (inches)	2.7

(Solmat3.to1)

Alpha=90,Beta=65 50 MPH Peak Gusts
        Max Stress (psi)   20992
        Max Displacement (inches)   1.8
Gravity Only - Facing Horizon
        Max Stress (psi)   5325
        Max Displacement (inches)   .20

Gravity Only - Stow
        Max Stress (psi)   8879
        Max Displacement (inches)   .81

The torque tube is made from ASTM A53B steel. This material has a yield strength of 35 ksi and a tensile strength of 60 ksi (ASM Metals Handbook Volume 1, Page 332, **Table 7**). The trusses are made from ASTM A36 steel. This material has a yield strength of 36 ksi and a tensile strength of 58 ksi (Marks' Standard Handbook for Mechanical Engineers, Eighth Edition, Page 6-27, Table 11a).

(Solmat3.to1)

Table 3-1 50 mph Wind Loads

SOLMAT Heliostat

Operational Wind Loads - 50 MPH Peak Gusts

Coefficients (tabulated values)

	Peak Load Coefficients						Mean Load Coefficients		
	Fx Max	Fz Max	MHy Max	Mz Max	Stow		Fx Max	Fz Max	MHy Max
a	90.00	30.00	30.00	90.00	0.00		90.00	30.00	30.00
b	0.00	0.00	0.00	65.00	0.00		0.00	0.00	0.00
Fx	4.00	2.10	2.10	3.70	0.60		2.00	1.00	1.00
Fz	1.00	2.80	2.80	0.50	0.90		0.30	1.35	1.35
MHy	0.25	0.60	0.60	0.15	0.20		0.02	0.25	0.25
Mz	0.29	0.06	0.06	0.70	0.02		0.00	0.00	0.00

Input Parameters		Output Parameters (calculated values)
Heliostat Center Height (ft)	21.63	Mean Wind at Height of Wind Measurem
Horizontal Chord Length (ft)	63.35	Mean Wind at Height of Dish Center (mp
Vertical Chord Length (ft)	42.26	Equivalent Heliostat Area (ft^2)
Porosity Area Ratio	0.80	Dynamic Pressure (lb/ft^2)
Wind Peak Gust (mph)	50.00	
Height of Wind Measurement (ft)	32.80	
Power Law Exponent	0.17	

Forces (calculated values) *Forces in Lbs, Moments in Ft-Lbs*

	Peak Loads						Mean Loads		
	Fx Max	Fz Max	MHy Max	Mz Max	Stow		Fx Max	Fz Max	MHy Max
a	90.00	30.00	30.00	90.00	0.00		90.00	30.00	30.00
b	0.00	0.00	0.00	65.00	0.00		0.00	0.00	0.00
Fx	18590.38	9759.95	9759.95	17196.10	2788.56		9295.19	4647.59	4647.59
Fz	4647.59	13013.26	13013.26	2323.80	4182.83		1394.28	6274.25	6274.25
MHy	49101.83	117844.40	117844.40	29461.10	39281.47		3928.15	49101.83	49101.83
Mz	85383.28	17665.51	17665.51	206097.57	5888.50		0.00	0.00	0.00

Fx	= Drag Force	a = Elevation Angle
Fz	= Lift Force	b = Azimuth Angle
MHy	= Elevation Moment	
Mz	= Azimuth Moment	

(Solmat3.to1)

Table 3-2 90 mph Wind Loads

SOLMAT Heliostat
Survival Wind Loads - 90 MPH Peak Gusts

Coefficients (tabulated values)

	Peak Load Coefficients					Mean Load Coefficients		
	Fx Max	Fz Max	MHy Max	Mz Max	Stow	Fx Max	Fz Max	M
a	90.00	30.00	30.00	90.00	0.00	90.00	30.00	
b	0.00	0.00	0.00	65.00	0.00	0.00	0.00	
Fx	4.00	2.10	2.10	3.70	0.60	2.00	1.00	
Fz	1.00	2.80	2.80	0.50	0.90	0.30	1.35	
MHy	0.25	0.60	0.60	0.15	0.20	0.02	0.25	
Mz	0.29	0.06	0.06	0.70	0.02	0.00	0.00	

Input Parameters		Output Parameters (calculated val
Heliostat Center Height (ft)	21.63	Mean Wind at Height of Wind Meas
Horizontal Chord Length (ft)	63.35	Mean Wind at Height of Dish Center
Vertical Chord Length (ft)	42.26	Equivalent Heliostat Area (ft^2)
Porosity Area Ratio	0.80	Dynamic Pressure (lb/ft^2)
Wind Peak Gust (mph)	90.00	
Height of Wind Measurement (ft)	32.80	
Power Law Exponent	0.17	

Forces (calculated values) *Forces in Lbs, Moments in Ft-Lbs*

	Peak Loads					Mean Loads		
	Fx Max	Fz Max	MHy Max	Mz Max	Stow	Fx Max	Fz Max	M
a	90.00	30.00	30.00	90.00	0.00	90.00	30.00	
b	0.00	0.00	0.00	65.00	0.00	0.00	0.00	
Fx	60232.82	31622.23	31622.23	55715.36	9034.92	30116.41	15058.21	
Fz	15058.21	42162.98	42162.98	7529.10	13552.39	4517.46	20328.58	
MHy	159089.94	381815.87	381815.87	95453.97	127271.96	12727.20	159089.94	
Mz	276641.83	57236.24	57236.24	667756.14	19078.75	0.00	0.00	

Fx	= Drag Force	a = Elevation Angle
Fz	= Lift Force	b = Azimuth Angle
MHy	= Elevation Moment	
Mz	= Azimuth Moment	

23

(Solmat3.tol)

3.5   Heliostat Structure Design Revision

The diameter of the torque-tube was increased from 18" to 24" after excessive sag was found with the first heliostat. Additional information on the 24"design is shown below. The heliostat under gravity only, with 50 MPH gusts in two orientations, and 90 mph gusts in stow was evaluated. The worst gravity sag due to the structure only (not including drive) is 0.8" in the stow position. The cross braces and connecting truss in the center reduce this sag to 0.2" in the vertical position (facing horizon). The worst stresses are under 50 MPH wind at an azimuth angle of 65 degrees. This condition puts an azimuth twisting moment on the system and produces torque tube stresses of 21,000 pi. The material has a yield stress of 35,000 psi so we should be fine. A modal analysis on the system (not including drive stiffness) was also performed. This analysis showed that the first three modes are torque tube bending modes with frequencies ranging from 3.6 Hz to 4.2 Hz. The fourth mode was the first torque tube torsional mode with a frequency of 5 Hz. The results of the analysis are summarized in the table below.

Parameter	*Extreme Value*	*Condition*
Gravity Sag	.8 in (Torque Tube End)	Stow
Stress	21,000 psi (Torque Tube at Drive Attachment)	50 MPH Wind Gust at 65 Degree Azimuthal Angle
Displacement	2.6 in (Upper Comer of Truss)	90 MPH Wind Gust in Stow
Frequency	3.6 Hz	First Torque Tube Bending Mode
Frequency	5.0 Hz	First Torque Tube Torsional Mode

3.6   Control System Development

A heliostat control system was developed in Phase II based on design concepts and criteria developed during Phase I of the program. The system is based on an off-the-shelf microprocessor-type controller and simple, single-phase AC motors controlled in an on-off manner. The orientation of the heliostat is measured by counting the motor revolutions using a simple optical encoder and projecting the motor motion through the gear train to calculate the motion of the heliostat. Solid-state relays are used to turn the motors on and off, and mechanical relays are used to reverse the directions of the motors under program control.

The heliostat control program is very simple. Essentially, all the heliostat controller does is position the heliostat to a commanded position based on communication with the central control computer. A version of the software was developed that allows autonomous tracking of the system, but in the Phase II system, all decisions about movement are made in the central computer. The details of the control hardware and software are contained in the Heliostat Control System Description and Manual (Revision 2, 22 April 1998).

(Solmat3.to1)

Components of the control system were built into a "brassboard" system in March 1997, including the control board and early encoders. These were tested and proved in the lab before production of hardware for the four heliostats was begun. Also, a wind meter and network interface was developed to monitor the wind for high-wind alarms and to enable communication between a PC-based control computer and a string of multiple heliostats. Finally, a simple user interface for the PC-based control computer was developed, based on the earlier dual-module heliostat control interface. It should be noted that this program was aimed at development of the heliostat itself, therefore, development of a central control program and user interface was beyond the scope of the program.

3.7   Heliostat Drive System

3.7.1   Introduction

The drive system for the heliostat is an important cost component, comprising up to 1/3 of the cost of the heliostat. SAIC is applying a significant effort to reduce drive costs for both our dish and heliostat systems. We are investigating several avenues of potential cost reduction for drive systems. SAIC has set a cost goal of $3,500 for the drive in order to make our heliostat and dish products cost competitive. We are working with conventional drive manufacturers that have fabricated concentrator drive systems previously, such as Winsmith, as a baseline approach for a drive cost reduction. Under contract to Sandia Laboratories, SAIC is also developing an advanced drive system based on large diameter wheels for gear reduction. SAIC's subcontractor, Boeing, has been investigating drive systems through their subsidiary, Dodge Engineering. A final decision on drive systems for dish and heliostat products has not been made at this time. The remainder of this section is devoted to a description of the Boeing/Dodge drive activity under the SolMaT program.

3.7.2   Boeing Drive Approach

Boeing, under subcontract to SAIC, has supported their efforts to identify ways to reduce costs associated with the manufacture and assembly of heliostats to be used in future commercial solar power plants based on central receiver technology. Boeing's scope has included an assessment of Boeing capabilities relative to providing a cost-effective gear drive system for heliostat application.

Given that the azimuth and elevation drive units represent a substantial portion of the overall cost of a heliostat, Boeing has committed to exploring its company-wide capabilities to determine if resources are available to define a cost-effective alternative. Because of schedule and budget constraints, the approach has been to not attempt a design from scratch but instead to determine if a configuration relying primarily on existing Boeing products could be defined. Because the primary challenge in this area is relative to the mechanical gearing aspects, the emphasis under this task has been on exploring available options for meeting the SAIC-provided requirements specific to the baseline multi-facet heliostat concept (~170 sq. meters). Given this objective, Boeing has worked closely with Dodge Engineering, a part of Boeing's Automation Division which also includes Allen-Bradley and Reliance. Discussions with Dodge personnel have been on going since early in the program, and the following summarizes activity to date and current recommendations.

25

3.7.3 Background

In 1995, Boeing initiated an internally-funded investigation with a long-term objective of identifying a cost-effective heliostat gear drive system that uses "off-the-shelf" components. At that time, Boeing chose first to explore capabilities and product lines within the corporation to determine if viable options were available. This led to initial discussions and ultimately a long standing relationship with Dodge Engineering. (Dodge is a segment of Rockwell International having extensive capability in the design and manufacture of gearing products). Working with Dodge personnel, Rocketdyne was able to develop a concept for a drive system comprised of existing gear products, each of which are available in a range of sizes. **(Figure 3-13).**

During the initial assessment of this concept, it was generally accepted that many of the traditional heliostat performance requirements (e.g., tracking and slew speeds, backlash, etc.) could easily be met with the Dodge components. The primary emphasis, therefore, was on trying to better understand load handling capability of these units. Given the tremendous gravity and wind loads associated with the larger size heliostats, the initial concern was whether the output stage Torque Arm Reducer had sufficient strength in its gear teeth and casing. (The gearbox case is composed of two halves-attached together by dowel pins and bolts and accurately assembled to insure proper gear mesh and efficient operation. Any relative motion between the two case halves will cause the gears to shift from their original position and affect the performance of the unit.) For an initial assessment of component performance, Dodge personnel analytically projected the reducer's load handling capability by correcting catalog ratings using an assumed heliostat duty cycle. With this approach, it was concluded that "off-the-shelf" Dodge components capable of accommodating these larger heliostats (i.e., > 70 sq. meters) were available but not practical. Although the input and intermediate stages are relatively compact and inexpensive, the output stage necessary would be both extremely large and costly. Therefore, the concept did not appear to represent a cost-effective solution for the heliostats of this size with the wind loads being considered. At that point, alternatives for proceeding were identified and considered. It was ultimately decided that, because of the uncertainties in the analytical projections, a prudent next step would be to assess component performance capabilities in a laboratory environment. This, then, became the base for the Phase 2 activities reported herein.

Figure 3-13. Proposed Drive Configuration

Proposed Drive Configuration

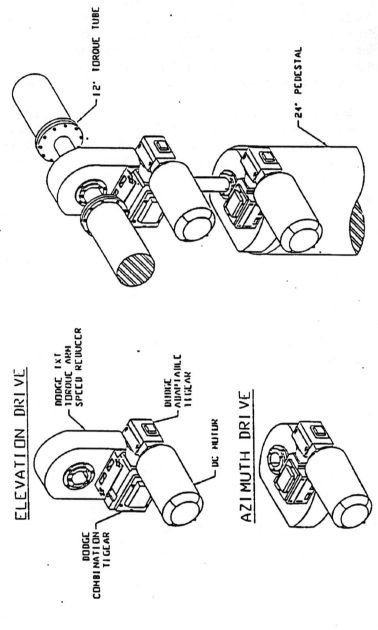

ELEVATION DRIVE

AZIMUTH DRIVE

12" TORQUE TUBE

24" PEDESTAL

DODGE TXT TORQUE ARM SPEED REDUCER

DODGE ADAPTABLE TIGEAR

DC MOTOR

DODGE COMBINATION TIGEAR

PROPRIETARY - DODGE

Rockwell Aerospace
Rocketdyne

27

3.7.4 Phase 2 Assessment of Performance Capability

Objective:
The purpose of this phase of the evaluation was to determine, via laboratory testing, true load handling capability of selected Dodge gearing components.

General Approach:
Because of funding constraints, testing of multiple units was not feasible. It was, therefore, decided that sizes selected for testing should be somewhat consistent with envisioned cost targets for heliostat drive systems. It was never expected that these smaller sizes would be able to accommodate the tremendous loads associated with the larger (i.e., > 150 sq. meter) heliostats. Instead, once strength characteristics were determined, this information could then be used to see if it made sense to consider smaller size heliostats and/or reduced wind loads such that these "off-the-shelf" components could be utilized. With this logic, Size 8 and 9 torque arm reducers TXT 8 and TXT 9) were selected as viable candidates for testing under high load conditions. As a prelude, smaller size components (TXT 4) were tested in the Dodge laboratory to make an initial assessment of anticipated performance.

Testing at Dodge:
The Dodge laboratory facilities in Greenville, South Carolina did not have the ability to test to failure the component sizes being considered for heliostat use. The Dodge personnel did, however, perform preliminary testing on smaller units to get an early indication of margins to failure relative to catalog ratings. Initial test results were better than anticipated with the TXT 4 component accommodating up to almost four times its rated capacity without failure.

Testing at Sandia National Laboratory:
Given the encouraging results from these initial tests conducted at the Dodge facilities, it was decided that additional testing on larger size components should be performed. Because of the much higher loads involved, Sandia National Laboratory's support was requested. Following a series of telecons and meetings between Rocketdyne, Dodge, and Sandia personnel, it was agreed that hardware to be tested would be configured and delivered to Sandia for testing. In early 1997, Dodge personnel assembled and shipped the following:

- 2 separate TXT 8 assemblies (torque arm reducer and associated input & intermediate stages)

- 2 separate TXT 9 assemblies (torque arm reducer and associated input & intermediate stages)

The following is a brief description of the testing performed.

The first series of tests were conducted in May, 1997. At that time, it was decided that, because of schedule and funding constraints, only the size 8 unit would be evaluated. Although the Dodge TXT gear reducer is designed to be mounted in a number of different positions depending on the application, modifications to the TXT gear box (e.g., drilling and tapping holes on the bottom side of the gear box) were needed to allow mounting the gear box to the interface plate in preparation for testing. Also, prior to mounting the gearbox to the interface plate and prior to

28

installing the torque arm in the output shaft, gearbox-housing bolts were re-torqued to 3120 in-lbs. Once these initial setups were completed, a series of tests, designed to evaluate torque and overturning moment load handling capabilities, were initiated.

Torque Tests:

The purpose of the torque tests was to evaluate torsional deflections in the gear reducer output shaft, deflections of the gearbox housing in the vicinity of the output shaft bearings, and overall load handling ability. To accomplish this, a test fixture was designed and fabricated to allow controlled forces to be applied to the Dodge gear reducer. (The load was applied as a symmetrical couple load to prevent any bending moment loads on the output shaft.) A total of six torque tests were performed on the Dodge TXT 8 gear reducer.

Instrumentation for the testing included strain gages, displacement gages, and actuators with built-in load and displacement capabilities. The strain gages were located on the casing and radially about the gear box flange, and displacement gages were used for measuring slippage between the two casing halves and for measuring rotational displacement of the shaft near its exit from the gear box flange.

It should be noted that the recorded strains were not particularly large. In addition, the maximum observed shaft rotation was 2.66 degrees, and the slippage measured between the two gearbox casing sections was minimal. (Maximum slippage was approximately 0.016 inches and returned to within 0.001 - 0.004 inches of its original position when unloaded.)

Overturning Moment Test:

The TXT 8 reducer was also tested in a base mount-overturning configuration. These tests were conducted to measure gearbox case deflections and slippage between the two case halves when subjected to extreme moment loads. Although instrumentation was essentially the same, minor adjustments in test setup were necessary. These included the use of 1) a single actuator to apply the force, 2) a Patriot gage to measure translational displacement, and a Kevlar strap to apply force to the top of the shaft. In this series of tests, the maximum force applied was 15,000 lb.

From this series of tests, it was determined that strain values obtained were insignificant, and there was no visual damage to the reducer. It was decided that this unit should be returned to Dodge for inspection of internal parts prior to proceeding with additional testing.

Following this inspection, it was agreed that additional tests that better defined failure points and mechanisms were needed. Therefore, a second series of tests was planned and conducted. Because the primary areas of interest were gear teeth and casing strength, the objective of these tests was to test to failure. In September, 1997, a second TXT 8 reducer was assembled in a side mount overturning test configuration. The purpose this time was to determine the failure load and the failure locations when using the L-shaped side mount bracket system. Instrumentation was similar to that used previously. The strain gages were located on the reducer case and radially about the gearbox flange. The reducer was loaded twice, and, during the second loading, failure of the casing was observed. Data and associated plots are included in Sandia's report. It should be noted, however, that a force of approximately 39,000 lb. (at a distance of ~2.25 ft.)

(Solmat3.to1)

was applied to the reducer through the shaft before failure occurred. The unit was returned to Dodge for further assessment.

Conclusions and Recommendations:

Based upon these very preliminary test results, it is difficult to reach definitive conclusions regarding concept viability. From a technical perspective, there is enough information available to be encouraged that the Dodge components may represent an "off-the-shelf" drive system alternative for smaller size heliostats. The TXT 8 reducer has demonstrated a load handling capability of up to almost 90,000 ft.-lbs., and, therefore, it is conceivable that heliostats up to ~ 85 - 95 sq. meters in surface area could be accommodated with these units. (Second generation heliostats, tested in the early 1980's, were approximately 50 - 60 sq. meters in size and had corresponding 90 mph wind load moments of -20,000 - 30,000 ft. lbs. The larger size heliostats (i.e., > 150 sq. meters) of today are more likely to be in the range of ~ 150,000 - 180,000 ft. lbs.) A prudent next step, to better understand technical capabilities, would be to install and test these components on an actual heliostat. One possibility for proceeding would be to scale down one of today's larger size heliostat design concepts such that the gravity and wind loads are within the desired load range and then build and field test this smaller size system using the Dodge components. Another option would be to modify and field test an existing smaller size heliostat (possibly at Solar Two or at Sandia.) The heliostat test series would be much broader in scope than the one just completed and would include an overall assessment of drive system performance.

The size of the heliostat and drive components selected for field-testing should be based upon an optimization activity that identifies the most cost-effective combination for these smaller size heliostats. Additional laboratory testing on smaller size gear components is likely to be needed to further evaluate strength characteristics and ensure that the appropriate size gear components are selected for a given heliostat size. Available component options and their associated costs should be obtained directly from Dodge personnel, and these discussions should also include an assessment of sensitivity of individual component costs to volume rate assumptions. It should also be noted that, if there is no requirement for "face-down" stowage, the elevation drive could be simplified to a linear jack screw device, a cheaper alternative to the concept proposed herein. (The Dodge components could still be used for the azimuth drive.)

In conclusion, continued investigation in this area appears to be warranted for those who might be interested in smaller size (i.e., < 95-sq. meter) heliostats. Unit area costs ($/sq.meter) competitive with other options available today are likely to be achievable. While these anticipated costs may not necessarily be within desired levels for long-term, high volume commercial application, they may be attractive enough to support early market entry. Direct contact and continued discussion with Dodge personnel to explore potential options is highly encouraged.

3.7   Heliostat Installation Experience

SAIC installed four heliostats under Phase II of SolMaT. One heliostat was installed at the NREL Mesa Top Facilities Area in Golden, Colorado, the second at the National Solar Thermal Test Facility at Sandia Laboratories in Albuquerque, New Mexico, and the third and fourth at

30

Solar Two in Daggett, California. The heliostat at NREL was installed primarily as a checkout test for fit-up of components and for the control and tracking system. The 18" torque tube included on this heliostat was found to be inadequate for maintaining the structural stiffness needed for optical accuracy. Therefore, steel bar was used for reinforcement on the torque tube near the drive to increase stiffness. Diagonal struts were also installed from near the end of the torque tube up to the inside vertical truss at the top of the heliostat, to help support the tips of the torque tubes. On the subsequent heliostats, the torque tube diameter was increased to 24" to increase torque tube stiffness. Some minor problems were incurred during assembly of this heliostat, and the design drawings were modified to reflect the changes that were necessary.

The entire heliostat structure, including the drive was assembled on the ground and then lifted onto the pedestal for mounting. Some minor problems were found with the control system, primarily in the area of encoders and sensors. Once those problems were solved, the heliostat was able to track a target mounted on an adjacent fence with good accuracy. Some meteorological equipment and strain gages were subsequently installed at this facility to measure the strain in heliostat components as a function of wind speed. This test, which is being conducted by NREL, will help to determine actual wind loads incurred on heliostat as a function of wind velocity.

The heliostat installed at Sandia Laboratories in Albuquerque was installed primarily to evaluate the optical performance of the heliostat. This heliostat was installed with a focus control system to compare the optics of the unit with and without focus control. A beam characterization system was used to evaluate the image of the heliostat on a target mounted on the tower. The heliostat was canted on the ground using a laser system in an experiment to determine if off-sun canting of the heliostat was possible. When the heliostat was brought on sun, it was found that additional adjustment of the facets was required in order to improve the optics of the heliostat. On-sun canting was accomplished to reduce the spot size and to reduce the effects of off-axis aberration, which was causing a dual image on the target. The optics were improved, however the dual image continues to be an issue for short slant ranges. Because the heliostat is so large, dual images are unavoidable during certain times of day and certain times of year.

The third and fourth heliostats were installed at Solar Two to demonstrate their performance in conjunction with an actual central receiver power system. The installation of these heliostats was delayed several times due to corrosion failure of some of the mirror facets incurred from contamination during shipping, delays in obtaining a building permit by SAIC's subcontractor, Bechtel, and excessively high winds in the spring time when the heliostats were to be mounted on the pedestals. Bechtel was subcontracted to do the field wiring and install the pedestals for these two units. Significant delays were also incurred with these items.

The high winds for a long time period are probably the most troubling issue for future installations of heliostat fields. With the current system of hanging the heliostats with a crane, the heliostats cannot be hung at a wind speed over 5-10 miles per hour. An optional method of installing the heliostats is recommended in order to increase the wind speed threshold where installation can be achieved.

The two units at Solar Two are installed and operational, but have not as yet been tested for optical performance. These tests are anticipated to be performed by SunLab personnel.

(Solmat3.to1)

3.9 Heliostat Canting

As mentioned in the previous section, the heliostat was canted using an experimental, laser-based system. To perform the canting, an analysis of the heliostat optics is performed for the distance to the target. Theoretical offsets are then determined for each of the three mounting points of each facet to position that facet correctly to reflect light to the target. Then a laser is set up on the drive of the heliostat, producing a flat plane of light over the heliostat surface. This serves as a reference plane. Finally, measuring devices are used to measure the offset of each facet mount from the reference plane, and the mounts are adjusted to give the desired values. The method was used successfully on each of the heliostats, although corrections were required to compensate for deflections of the structure. The same approach was also used to implement the corrections. In addition, the laser plane system was used to make measurements of the heliostat shape as it moved through its range of motion in order to verify design predictions for the system.

3.10 References

Heliostat Control System Description and Operator Manual, Revision 2, Roger Davenport, SAIC Energy Products Division, 22 April 1998.

(Solmat3.to1)

4.0 MANUFACTURING TECHNOLOGY EVALUATION

4.0 Manufacturing Technology Evaluation

The manufacturing of thin foil stretched membrane mirror facets can be separated into four distinctive elements. Essentially, a facet consists of a welded stainless steel ring, onto which two separate thin foil stainless steel membranes are stretched and then attached by roll resistance welding. By using this method, a structurally stiff, optically flat facet can be achieved. The finished component is a 6-inch deep two-sided disc-like structure, upon which a reflective surface can be applied. A summary of the four elements and the sequential manufacturing process steps associated with fabricating a stretched membrane heliostat facet are outlined in the following subsections.

4.1 Ring Production

4. 1.1 Ring, Rolling/Manufacture

A main component of the SAIC 3.0 stretched membrane mirror module is the facet ring assembly. Prior to the SolMaT initiative, this assembly was constructed of three 120-degree, M6 x 4.4 structural steel I-beam segments. These segments were rolled by an outside vendor, then shipped to our facility and welded together using standard MIG welding and fixturing techniques. These standard processes have proven effective in producing a uniform planner ring assembly onto which tensioned membranes can be installed and then attached via a specialized roll resistance welding process. Under the SolMaT initiative, the material and labor costs associated with producing ring assemblies were held to further scrutiny. A change was made to a channel design, which is bent from sheet metal coil stock. The material was changed to Type 409 stainless steel to improve weldability and eliminate the need for painting. To decrease ring rolling costs, large production ring-rolling scenarios were submitted to outside vendors for quotation. It was found that vendors specializing in structural steel beam rolling could not reduce overall ring costs significantly given the requirements for increased production. For example, a ring segment produced for $235.00 in low production quantities saw only a 10% cost reduction when produced in production quantities of 5,000 segments per year. The conclusions that were drawn for large production ring rolling scenarios under the SolMaT initiative were as follows:

a.   In order to produce ring assemblies at reduced cost, an in-house production channel forming and ring-rolling capability would have to be implemented. This may include the development or modification of existing equipment to improve process time and insure segment accuracy.

b.   In order to reduce material handling and process time, rings can be produced in 180-degree segments. This reduces the welding labor and materials required to fabricate the segments into a completed ring assembly.

33

4.1.2 Surface Preparation

To aid in the attachment of the foil membranes to the facet ring, the ring flanges must be free of surface scale, dirt and minor imperfections. Previously, this surface preparation was accomplished by a labor-intensive grinding process. Under the SolMaT initiative alternative, less-costly methods were explored. Parallel gap welding experiments were performed to attach .003" HH stainless steel material to untreated and sandblasted .125" mild steel and stainless steel flange samples. Under pull testing, the untreated mild steel flange surfaces did not demonstrate welded metallurgical bonds. However, a lightly treated stainless surface produced satisfactory welds. Also, a sandblasted mild steel flange could adequately support the flange-to-foil attachment.

4.1.3 Facet Mounting/Adjustment

The installation of the facets onto the structure is accomplished by the following method. Each facet has three specially designed brackets that are attached to the facet ring wall at 120-degree intervals. The facet is lowered into place and secured to mounting holes located on the structure. An ideal facet-mounting bracket would allow for simple facet installation and also allow for easy facet canting the minor facet alignments which are necessary to insure optimum receiver efficiency. The bracket must be cost effective, yet provide a fair range of motion without transferring unwanted loads into the module itself (non-uniform canting loads may adversely affect the optical quality of the mirror module.) Under the SolMaT initiative, concepts for a simplified mounting bracket have undergone the rigors of a Design for Manufacturability (DMFA) process. The result has produced a mounting bracket that is slightly lower in cost than the previous design, and that provides for simpler facet installation and canting, thereby lowering labor costs associated with these operations.

4.2 Membrane Production

The present manufacturing process for producing a circular .003" thin foil membranes involves roll-resistance seam welding of 24 inch wide coil stock. The coil stock is pulled to length and then cut. By welding several cut sheets together, an 11' x 11' flat sheet of .003" material is produced. The present process uses a uni-directional seam welder positioned on an overhead rail system. Below the seam welder, a vacuum table with a grounding electrode accommodates two sheets of the cut material. Sheet by sheet, the material is roll-resistance seam welded with a 0.5" overlap and rolled onto a storage tube. Once the membrane has the proper number of welded panels, the storage tube is removed from the welder and stored on a rack. The process begins again until a sufficient quantity of membranes has been produced. This method was specially designed to produce overlapping metallurgical welds in thin foil material. Further speed enhancements can be made by designing a bi-directional or multiple seam cascade welder. A cascade welder would have several weld heads that would operate in parallel, to weld a continuous sheet of membrane material the width of the facets. Also, pre-cutting the finished membrane to a circular diameter directly downstream of the welding process has reduced production time. In a high production scenario, a fully automated welding and cutting table would be designed for this purpose. This would further reduce production time, producing membranes on a just in time basis, thereby eliminating the need to store membranes before use.

4.3   Facet Assembly

4.3.1   Facet Fixturing

The facet ring assembly and membranes are brought together into a tensioning fixture for final assembly. The facet ring is installed into the membrane-tensioning fixture and leveled. Membranes are installed both top and bottom, where they are tensioned by specially designed pneumatic clips. The tensioned membranes are then welded to the facet ring. The completed unit is trimmed and removed from the fixture in preparation for the application of glass mirror tiles. Prior to the SolMaT initiative, many of these process steps were accomplished manually.

4.3.2   Tensioning

On previous units, the tensioning of the membranes required the manual attachment of 120 pre-cut non-reusable tensioning strips. These strips were attached to the top and bottom of each membrane via a labor-intensive manual seam welding process. A new semi-automated production tensioning method has been implemented during the SolMaT initiative. This process incorporates the use of 276 specially designed reusable tensioning clips, which are pneumatically actuated. The prototype semi-automated clip assembly was fabricated and tested. The results have proven to be a ma or breakthrough in reducing the labor and materials cost of this process. A full scale-tensioning fixture incorporating this semi-automated concept has since been fabricated and used in production. This is a precursor to a fully automated concept slated for high production scenarios. The high production concept will utilize a fully automated pneumatically operated gripper, which will require no touch labor to engage the membranes. A photo of the tool is shown in **Figure 4-1.**

4.3.3   Welding

To attach the pre-tensioned membranes to the facet ring, a roll-resistance seam welding method is used. During the seam welding process, weld current was previously passed through the membrane and into the grounded facet ring assembly. The resistance interface between the stainless steel membrane and facet ring produces heat, thereby effecting a weld. This method has proven adequate in the past, but there have been inherent flaws in this process.

(Solmat3.to1)

Figure 4-1. Tooling Photograph

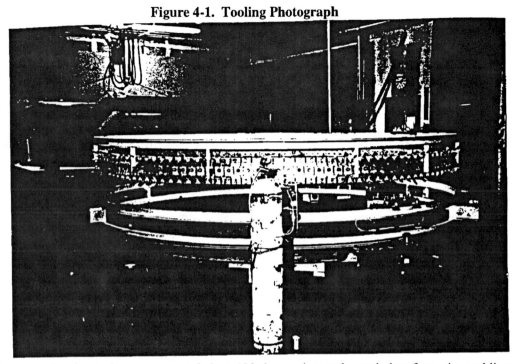

In the past, the facet ring was grounded at 120-degree intervals, and therefore, the welding resistance varied in relation to the distance between the grounding point and the weld head. Under the SolMaT effort, a more effective concept known as parallel-gap welding was designed and implemented. This concept uses dual welding electrodes/wheels spaced several inches apart. The electrode wheels are electrically insulated from each other, thereby allowing the wheels to be opposite in polarity. Current flows from the positive electrode/wheel, through the material, and back into the negative electrode/wheel (hence the acronym parallel-gap welding.) This method produces more uniform welds and at higher weld speeds than the previous method. For large-scale production, a higher pulse rate-welding controller may have to be considered to achieve welding speeds capable of meeting high production goals. Exploration of alternative membrane to ring attachment methodology is an ongoing process, as technology advancements in the welding and adhesive attachment technologies may ultimately provide a more cost effective solution for high-production scenarios.

4.4 Mirror Tiles

The original dual module heliostat used a polymer film reflector surface (ECP-305). However, polymer reflectors have shown limited lifetimes in the field, and suffer from high cost. Therefore, since the prototype dual module heliostat was installed, SAIC has experimented with the use of glass mirrors on stretched membrane reflectors, with excellent success. For instance, the dish/Stirling systems produced by SAIC for the Utility-Scale Joint Venture Program (USJVP) employed 1.0 mm thick float glass mirrors. In the SolMaT program, investigations have continued in evaluation of mirror materials and application and adhesive technologies. As

(Solmat3.to1)

a result of these investigations, the following specifications have been selected for the glass mirrors of systems:

- 3/32" float glass
- 6-round-cut mirrors

Regarding mirror application, the investigations have identified the most cost-effective approach for production at 2,000 heliostats per year to be a robotic pick&place unit combined with automatic roll-coaters for adhesive application. The roll-coaters would apply a hot-melt, pressure-sensitive adhesive. In Phase II, a transfer sheet adhesive was used with manual mirror placement because of the cost associated with the above tooling.

4.5   Structure Fabrication

4.5.1   Truss Assembly Automated Tooling Concept

The truss assembly machining center is designed to automatically perform the cutting and drilling operations required to produce a completed component ready for installation **(Figure 4-2)**. The machining center is composed of two power feed roller conveyors, a high-speed cutting table and a drilling center capable of drilling multiple holes in one operation. Other features include a set of preprogrammed stops capable of stopping and clamping the truss beam at the specified location for cutting and drilling.

Principle of Operation:

The truss beam is loaded on the first conveyor and is then advanced to the cutoff saw for cutting the end brace. The stops and clamps, which are, controlled by a programmable controller accurately position the truss beam for its first cutting operation. The next step is to perform the center cut where the beam is cut into two pieces. Once this is completed, the front half of the truss beam is advanced to the drilling center. As it advances it is stopped along the way, again using preprogrammed stops and clamps to drill the holes in the top flanges of the beam. These holes are intended for mounting the cross truss assemblies and the facets. As the truss beam reaches its end, the final drilling operation is performed. A series of vertical holes drilled in the side angles intended for mounting the truss beam onto the torque tube flange. Once this is completed the beam is then moved to a deburring station (not shown in this tooling concept) for final deburring and inspection. In the mean time the second half of the beam is advanced forward until it reaches its final cutting position to cut the end brace. Next the beam is advanced to the drilling center. The first drilling operation would be to drill the vertical holes for flange mounting. And the final step is advancing the beam and drilling the side holes for mounting the cross truss assemblies. Finally, the beam advances to the deburring and inspection station, and the process is repeated again on another truss beam.

(Solmat3.to1)

Figure 4-2. Truss Assembly Automated Tooling

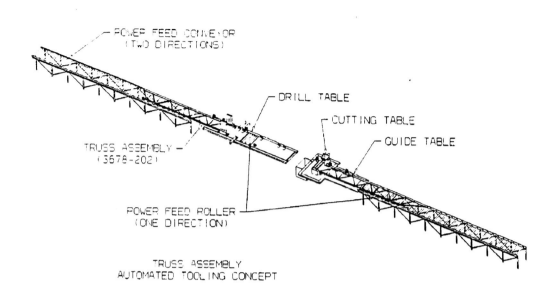

TRUSS ASSEMBLY
AUTOMATED TOOLING CONCEPT

4.5.2 Cross Truss Assemblies - Semi-Automated Tooling Concept

The weld fixtures for assembling the cross truss assemblies support a semi-automated process that includes some manual operations to complete the assembly **(Figure 4-3)**. The process uses a trunion mounted welding jig with fittings designed to accurately locate the various angle components. Once the parts are loaded and secured to the jig, welding operations are performed. The trunion mount has an electric motor to rotate the jig during the manual welding processes; however, robotic welding systems can be implemented to increase production capacity.

4.5.3 Torque Tube Assembly Semi-Automated Tooling Concept

The torque tube assembly consists of a standard pipe cut to length, a round flange mounted at one end and four square flanges mounted at pre-specified locations on the pipe **(Figure 4-4)**. The semi-automated tool designed to accomplish the task of assembling the torque tube consists of a simple fixture with V-block bearing that allows the pipe to rotate about its axis. On this fixture are flange locators used to accurately locate the square flanges on the pipe. The end flange is located using a special fixture that serves two purposes. The first is to locate the flange at the end of the pipe. The second is to rotate the pipe assembly during welding operation by using a variable speed motor and drive assembly.

38

Figure 4-3. Cross Truss Assembly Tooling Concept

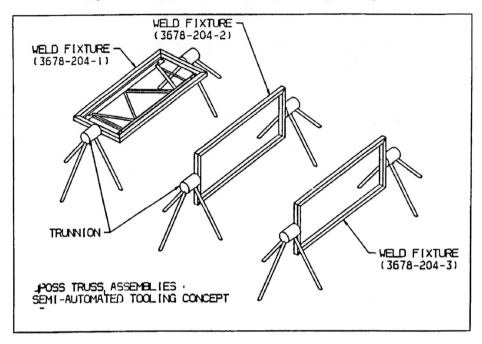

Figure 4-4. Torque Tube Assembly Semi-Automated Tooling Concept

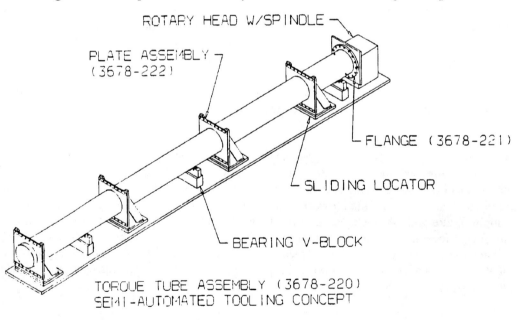

To complete a torque tube assembly, the round flange is mounted to the end fixture, and the four square flanges are then mounted on the corresponding flange locators. The pipe is next slid into place through the square flanges. Once all components are located in the correct places, tack welding is performed to lock the parts in place. The next step is to slide the flange locators away from the square flanges to allow the pipe assembly to rotate. A robotic welder is then used to weld the flanges in place as the pipe is rotated using the variable speed drive unit.

Introducing additional features such as automatically sliding the flange locators could further automate this process and adding more robotic weld heads to perform all the flange welds at once.

(Solmat3.to1)

5.0   MANUFACTURING PLANT DESIGN

As a means of tying together the investigations of manufacturing technologies for the various components of the heliostat, a plant design was developed for a facet manufacturing plant capable of producing 2,000 heliostats per year. With the multi-faceted heliostat design, this results in the following breakdown of production rates:

> 2,000 heliostats/year
> 44,000 mirror facets/year
> 6.1 facets/hour
> 144 facets/day with three shifts
> 44,000 facets/year

The design described is based on three-shift operation, to make the best use of the production equipment. The selected target production rate is six facets per hour, giving 10 minutes of process time per facet. Using this production rate, equipment was sized and production was balanced between the various stations within the plant. The resulting plant is shown in flowchart form in **Figure 5-1** and on physical layout in **Figure 5-2.** The plant design described is based on the double membrane facet design.

The top half of **Figure 5-1** shows the processes related to facet ring production. Sheet metal coil stock is used to form ring sections, and then ring halves are welded and prepared for assembly into facets. At the bottom of the figure, membrane production stations feed from the outside into centrally located facet assembly fixtures where the membranes are tensioned and attached to the rings. Finally, at the bottom of the figure, the finished facets have mirror tiles attached, and are loaded into containers for shipment to the heliostat installation location. The time for each process step is shown in minutes on **Figure 5-1.** The actual times for each fabrication step in Phase II of SolMaT are shown in **Table 5-1.**

5.1   Truss Modification

The current plan is to purchase standard product trusses, which are modified for our use. The cross trusses are currently envisioned to be welded assemblies, and holes will have to be drilled in both to permit integration into the final assembly.

To perform these operations, approximately 900 square feet of floor space is estimated for Phase II and approximately 4,000 square feet is projected for Phase III. In addition to the standard tools needed to perform these operations, special tooling/fixturing can be designed and fabricated as needed for higher volume production. It is estimated that approximately five skilled and semi-skilled personnel will be required to support these modification tasks for Phase II, and approximately 38 skilled and semi-skilled personnel will be required for commercial production.

41

Figure 5-1. Fabrication Plant Flow chart

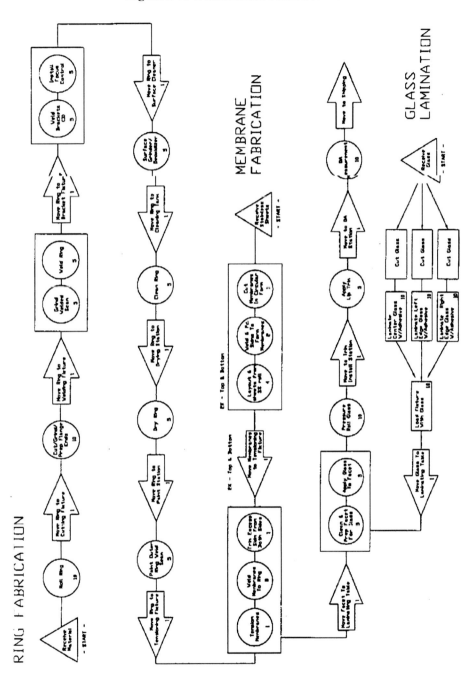

(Solmat3.to1)

Figure 5-2. Physical Layout of the Fabrication Plant

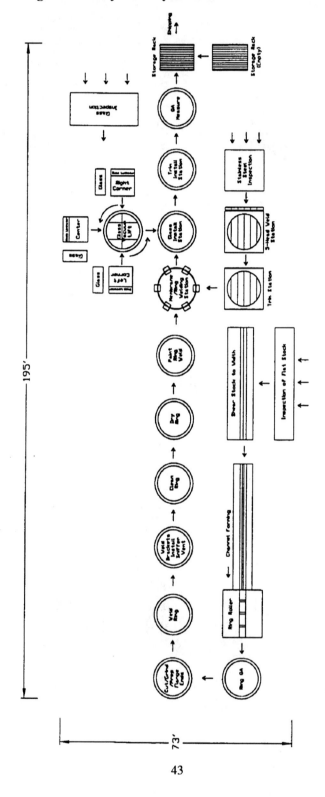

(Solmat3.to1)

Table 5-1. SolMaT Phase II Labor Actuals

Task #		Man-Hours	
1.	Inspect Segments	0.50	
2.	Grind ends of flanges	0.75	
3.	Load in welding fixture	0.75	
4.	Weld ring	1.50	
5.	Weld brackets	1.00	
6.	Install focus control	0.50	
7,	Surface preparation - grind	1.00	
8.	Clean ring	0.50	
9.	Load ring in tensioning fixture	1.00	
10.	Track welding heads	0.50	
11.	Cut membranes	1.00	
12.	Tension membranes	1.00	
13.	Weld membranes	0.50	
14.	Remove from tensioning fixture	0.50	
15.	Apply lip trim	0.50	
16.	QA Measurement	0.75	
17.	Mirror washing	1.00	
18.	Mirror lamination (adhesive)	1.50	
19.	Mirror install	3.00	
20.	Store	0.50	Total = 18.25 man-hours

5.2 Torque Tube Fabrication

The torque tubes are planned to be fabricated from purchased parts (pipe, flanges, plates, and end caps). These parts will have to be cut and welded together to produce the final torque tube assemblies.

To perform these operations, approximately 450 square feet of floor space is estimated to support Phase II and approximately 2,000 square feet will be needed to support Phase III. As needed, specialized fixtures and tooling can be developed to help ensure repeatability in the assemblies, quality, and reduced cost. The same skilled and semi-skilled personnel, mentioned in the truss modification, are available to support the torque tube fabrication.

5.3 Pedestal Fabrication

The pedestals are to be fabricated from purchased parts (pipe, flanges, sheet metal, re-bar, etc.). These parts will have to be cut, drilled and welded to produce final pedestal assemblies.

To perform these operations, approximately 450 square feet of floor space will be required. As previously mentioned for other structural components, specialized fixtures can be developed as needed, dependent upon volume production to help ensure repeatability in the assemblies, quality, and reduce cost. The same skilled and semi-skilled personnel, mentioned above, are available to support pedestal fabrication.

44

6.0   PRODUCTION COST ANALYSIS

6.1   Facet Production Costs

At the beginning of Phase II, a low-cost facet design had been identified using a single membrane of mild steel. This was found to be unworkable due to the imbalance of forces on the ring leading to poor optics, and the costs associated with coating the steel membranes to protect them against corrosion. Therefore, the program was continued using a design based on double-membrane mirror modules with stainless-steel membranes.

One of the major accomplishments of the Phase II program was implementation and testing of semi-automated fabrication tooling for the facets. This tooling allowed the man-hours per facet for facet manufacture to be reduced from 70 man-hours to 18.25 man-hours. The projections to full automation of the facet production process led to an estimate of 3.2 man-hours per facet at a production rate of 2,000 units per year.

6.2   Heliostat Production Costs

The following six pages **(Tables 6-1 and 6-2,** each three pages) contain a summary of an update to the production and installation costs for the SolMaT heliostat. The first three pages represent the actual cost of the Solar Two heliostat installations, and the final three pages are an extrapolation to 2,000 units per year with automated tooling. For the single-unit build, the heliostat cost is $100K, with $10K for engineering and overhead and $27K for installation giving a total installed cost of $138K. These systems were prototypes, installed in small quantities (1 and 2 at a site), so the costs are far from commercial values and are presented for reference purposes only.

At the 2,000 unit-per-year rate, the costs come down significantly. The heliostat fabrication costs are $21.5K, and about $5K is required for installation. Labor rates of $14 per hour were used for the fabrication and installation laborers, which is consistent with production employees in low-labor-rate areas such as the Southwest deserts. Engineering and overhead activities add about $0.2K, and capital equipment and profit of about $1.8K have been added to the cost in a commercial sales scenario, resulting in a total installed cost of $28.5K. This is about $157 per square meter of mirror area.

Looking at the cost estimates in detail, the first page is a summary of the fabrication, installation, engineering, and overhead costs associated with the installation. Bechtel estimates and actuals were used for the materials and equipment costs of the pedestal installation, wiring, and system lift (crane). SAIC labor estimates were used for each of those events. The second and third pages of each estimate are the materials costs and labor costs (both fabrication and installation). In all cases, the right-most column gives the justification or basis of each cost item. Note that in the materials and labor estimates, sub-totals are shown in bold print.

The predicted cost in the 2,000-unit/year scenario comes out to $157/m^2, which is high for market conditions. A couple of factors stand out. The first is the cost of trusswork and torque

45

tubes. These were estimated from a quote for similar trusswork for the JVP dish structure at a quantity of 500 systems. The total trusswork is about half of the heliostat materials cost. The second significant factor is high installation cost. For instance, the Bechtel estimate gives $850 for the wiring to each pedestal. This estimate is extrapolated from the two-heliostat installation at Solar 2, which required much more wiring than would be needed in a bare-field installation. Thus, the value seems high for the incremental cost of wiring 120 VAC and a single control cable to each heliostat. Finally, the estimate is more detailed than earlier ones, and includes more specific items. For instance, crane and boom truck rentals were not included in early estimates, and pedestal installation costs were underestimated.

Table 6-3 compares the cost estimate generated at the end of Phase I of the SolMaT program with the updated cost estimate. It needs to be noted that the Phase I estimate was based on a low-cost facet with only one membrane and carbon steel ring and membrane. Also, the truss costs and labor figures were estimated without good information. Finally, there were several items not included in the Phase I estimate, as noted above. As shown in the table, the materials costs for the Phase II system went up significantly. These costs were estimated from the quantity one actual data by applying discounts of 40% to purchased parts, 50% to fabricated components and electronics, and 75% to large steel components (torque tubes and pedestal).

The estimated cost for facets is $250 ($205 for materials, and about $45 for labor), which represents a large decrease from the Phase I estimate of $673. The decrease is mainly due to reduction in the estimated labor content of the facets from 19.8 man-hrs to 3.2 man-hrs. Since the efforts of the Phase II program were concentrated on facet cost reduction, this is a significant success even though the total heliostat cost is still too high.

46

SolMaT Heliostat Cost Summary
Single-Unit Build

		$ 137,802		Total Cost
			811	$/m^2
Component	Cost	Sub-Total	Cost/m^2	Basis
Heliostat		$ 99,982	588	
Materials	$ 63,532			see detail sheet
Fabrication Labor	$ 34,800			see detail sheet
Fabrication Supervision	$ 1,650			est. 1 hr/facet@$75/hr
Installation Costs		$ 27,320	161	
Soil Samples	$ 1,000			est. (Sandi D.)
Soil Analysis	$ 2,000			est. (Sandi D.)
Drill Hole and Set Pedestal	$ 5,440			Actual Solar 2 (Bechtel) mat'ls/equipment
Wiring to Pedestal	$ 7,140			Actual Solar 2 (Bechtel) mat'ls/equipment
Boom Truck Rental	$ 1,600			est. (4 days, $50/hr)
Crane to Install System	$ 2,040			Est Solar 2 (Bechtel) mat'ls/equipment
Installation Labor	$ 6,600			see detail sheet
Installation Supervision	$ 1,500			est. 20 hr/system @ $75/hr
Engineering		$ 4,500	26	
Foundation Design	$ 2,000			est. 20hrs @ $100/hr
Electrical Interface Design	$ 500			est. 5hrs @ $100/hr
Planning and Permits	$ 2,000			est. 20hrs @ $100/hr
Overhead		$ 6,000	35	
Project Management	$ 1,000			est. 10 hr/system @ $100/hr
Bookkeeping	$ 2,000			est. 40 hr/system @ $50/hr
Purchasing	$ 3,000			est. 40 hr/system @ $75/hr

(Solmat3.to1)

SolMaT Heliostat Materials Cost

Single-Unit Build

Total System Cost $ 63,532

Description	System	Assy	Sub-Assy	Unit Cost	Total Cost	Cost Basis
Drive Unit	1			8261	8261	
Flenders Drive		1		7500		Actual cost of refurbished drives for JVP Phase 2
Drive Motors		2		125		MMC 6135K12
Encoders		2		150		est. (Machined Parts ~ 90, elec. 15, assy 45)
Limit Switches		4		12		DigiKey 59066-030-ND, 57065-000-ND, 4/30/97
Junction Box		1		64		MMC 6918K75+6917K15
Misc. Hardware		1		100		MMC 7527K53x2; est.
Spool Plate, Pedestal-to-Drive	1			800	800	Silver Weibull quote, 4/30/97
Assembly Hardware	1			200	200	wag
Pedestal	1			5650	5650	Hales Eng. Invoice 11/4/97
Trusswork	1			39020	39020	
Torque Tubes		2		5485		Hales Eng. Invoice 11/17/97
Short Vertical Trusses		8		1100		est. from Hales Eng. Invoice 11/17/97
Long Vertical Trusses		8		1375		est. from Hales Eng. Invoice 11/17/97
Cross Trusses		15		550		Hales Eng. Invoice 11/17/97
Mirror Facets	22				9065	
Facet Trim		66		412		Actual JVP Phase 1; $/ft
Mirror Tile Set		1		0.26		Gump Glass Quote, 3/6/97
Mirror Adhesive		1		116		Est. from 3M phone Quote, 4/97
Facet Ring Assembly		1		43		
Facet Ring Segments			4	150		Roadrunner Quote, 11/97 (per Lem Tingley)
Mounting Brackets			3	30		Est.
Membrane Assembly		2		10		
201 SS foil			9	43		Actual JVP Phase 1; $/m^2
				5		
Control Box Assembly	1			486	486	
Enclosure		1		100		est.
Little PLC Controller		1		183		Zworld Actual, 4/30/97
Solid-State Relays		2		13		DigiKey CC1066-ND
Reversing Relays (3PDT)		2		19		MMC
24 VDC Power Supply		1		40		est.
Connectors		1		50		est.
Misc. Parts		1		50		est.
Cabling	1			50	50	est.

Mat'ls(1)

Table 6-1. Actual Cost of SolMaT Heliostats Installed at Solar 2 (page 3 of 3)

SolMaT Heliostat Labor Costs
Single-Unit Build

$ 60   Loaded Labor Rate

| | | | 690 | Total | $ 41,400 | |
Assembly/Task	Man-hrs	Qty Req'd	Total M-h	Cost	Sub-Total	Basis
Fabrication Labor			580		$ 34,800	-
Drive System						
Wire Drive Motors & Limits	20	1	20	1200		Est. from actual
Attach Spool Plate to Drive	4	1	4	240		Est. from actual
Mirror Facets						
Manufacture Mirror Facet	20	22	440	26400		Actuals for JVP
Apply Mirrors	4	22	88	5280		Actuals for JVP
Controls						
Assemble Control Box	20	1	20	1200		Est. from JVP/SolMaT actuals
Assemble Cables	8	1	8	480		Est. from JVP/SolMaT actuals
Installation Labor			110		$ 6,600	
Pedestal						
Install Pedestal	8	1	8	480		Est. from actuals
Drive						
Attach to Hub	4	1	4	240		Est. from actuals
Install System on Pedestal	8	1	8	480		Est. from actuals
Trusswork						
Assemble Torque Tubes	4	2	8	480		Est. from actuals
Assemble Vertical Trusses	4	8	32	1920		Est. from actuals
Assemble Cross Trusses	1	15	15	900		Est. from actuals
Mirror Facets						
Install Facets	1	22	22	1320		Est. from actuals
Adjust Facets	0.5	22	11	660		Est. from actuals
Controls						
Wire Control Box on Pedestal	2	1	2	120		Est. from actuals

Labor(1)

Printed 6/12/98

(Solmat3.to1)

Table 6-2. Estimated Cost of SolMaT Heliostats at 2000 Units per Year (page 1 of 3)

SolMaT Heliostat Costs
2000 Units/year

Reflective Area	170 sq m
Amortization Quantity	500 systems per location

Total: $ 28,442 $ 157 per sq m

Component	Cost	Subtotal	Cost/sq m	Cost Basis
Heliostat Fabrication		**21492**	**126**	
Materials	20264			**See detail sheet**
Labor	1154			**See detail sheet**
Supervision	75			1.5 supervisor @ $50/hr
Installation		**4941**	**29**	
Soil Analysis/Samples	6			Est (Sandi D.), amortized
Set Pedestal	2210			Bechtel est.
Field Wiring	850			Bechtel est.
Boom Truck	800			est. 2 days @ $50/hr
Crane	340			Bechtel est.
Labor	685			**See detail sheet**
Supervision	50			1 supervisor @50/hr
Engineering		**1**	**0.00**	
Foundation Design	0.2			est. 1 hr @ $100/hr, amortized
Electrical Interface Design	0.2			est. 1 hr @ $100/hr, amortized
Planning & Permits	0.2			est. 1 hr @ $100/hr, amortized
Overhead/Indirect		**200**	**1.2**	
Project Management	100			1 hr/system @ $100/hr
Bookkeeping	50			1 hr/system @ $50/hr
Purchasing	50			1 hr/system @ $50/hr
Capital Costs		**714**		$10 million, 7-yr straight-line
Profit		**1094**		4% of production costs

50

(Solmat3.to1)

SolMaT Heliostat Material Costs
2000 Units/year

Description	Qty Required System	Assy	Unit Cost	Assy Cost	Subtotal	Cost Basis
			Total	**$ 20,264**		
Drive Unit	1			4206	4206	
Drive System		1	3750	3750		50% for advanced drive
Drive Motors		2	75	150		–40% for volume
Encoders		2	90	180		–40% for volume
Limit Switches		4	7	28		–40% for volume
Junction Box		1	38	38		–40% for volume
Hardware		1	60	60		-40% for volume
Pedestal •	1		1413	1413	1413	-75% for volume
Assembly Hardware	1		120	120	120	-40% for volume
Trusswork	1			9764	9764	
Torque Tubes		2	1371	2742		-75% for volume
Short Vertical Trusses		8	275	2200		est. from SFI for 500 dishes
Long Vertical Trusses		8	344	2752		est. from SFI for 500 dishes
Cross Trusses		15	138	2070		est. from SFI for 500 dishes
Mirror Facets	22			205	4510	
Facet Segments		4	15	60		-50% for volume
SS Foil		18	2.3	41.4		-50% for volume
Mounting Brackets		3	5	15		-50% for volume
Mirror Adhesive		1	22	22		-50% for volume
Mirror Tile Set		1	58	58		-50% for volume
Trim		66	0.13	8.58		-50% for volume
Control Box	1			221	221	
Enclosure		1	60	60		-40% for volume
Little PLC Controller		1	60	60		Est. for Z-World
Solid-state Relays		2	6	12		-50% for circuit boards
Reversing Relays		2	10	20		-50% for circuit boards
24 VDC Power Supply		1	20	20		-50% for circuit boards
Connectors		2	12	24		-50% for circuit boards
Misc. Parts		1	25	25		-50% for circuit boards
Cabling	1		30	30	30	-40% for volume

(Solmat3.to1)

SolMaT Heliostat Labor Costs

2000 Units/year
Labor rate for dedicated production/installation labor in low labor-rate area

$ 14.00   Labor Rate (loaded)

Total: $ 1,839

Assembly/Task	Man-hrs	Qty Req'd	Total M-h	Cost	Subtotal	Basis of cost
Fabrication Labor			82		$ 1,154	
Manufacture Mirror Facets	3.2	22	70.4	985.6		full production equipment
Wire Motors & Limits	8	1	8	112.0		pre-wired
Assemble Control Box	2	1	2	28.0		printed circuit boards
Assemble Cables	2	1	2	28.0		pre-wired
Installation Labor			49		$ 685	
Install Pedestal	4	1	4	56.0		est. with improved tooling/fixtures
Attach Torque Tubes	2	2	4	56.0		est. with improved tooling/fixtures
Assemble Vertical Trusses	2	8	16	224.0		est. with improved tooling/fixtures
Assemble Cross Trusses	0.5	15	7.5	105.0		est. with improved tooling/fixtures
Install Facets	0.5	22	11	154.0		est. with improved tooling/fixtures
Align Facets	0.1	22	2.2	30.8		est. with improved tooling/fixtures
Install System on Pedestal	4	1	4	56.0		est. with improved tooling/fixtures
Wire Control Box	0.25	1	0.25	3.5		plug-together

52

(Solmat3.to1)

Table 6-3. Comparison of Phase I and Phase II Estimated Costs of SolMaT Heliostats

Comparison of Phase 1 and Phase 2 Heliostat Costs
2000 Units/year

	Phase 2	Phase 1	Difference	Explanation
Totals:	$ 28,442	$ 18,163	$ 10,279	
Heliostat Fabrication				
Materials	20264	12266	7998	Double-sided facets, higher costs for trusswork
Fabrication Labor	1154	495	659	Better estimate
Fabrication Supervision	75		75	Not included in Phase 1 est.
Installation				
Soil Analysis	6		6	Not included in Phase 1 est.
Drill and set pedestal	2210	1000	1210	Better estimate
Wiring to Pedestal	850	1000	-150	
Boom Truck Rental	800		800	Not included in Phase 1 est.
Crane to Install System	340		340	Not included in Phase 1 est.
Installation Labor	685	1250	-565	Better estimate
Installation Supervision	50		50	Not included in Phase 1 est.
Engineering				
Foundation Design	0.2		0.2	Not included in Phase 1 est.
Electrical Interface Design	0.2		0.2	Not included in Phase 1 est.
Planning and Permits	0.2		0.2	Not included in Phase 1 est.
Overhead/Indirect				
Project Management	100	35	65	Not included in Phase 1 est.
Bookkeeping	50		50	Not included in Phase 1 est.
Purchasing	50	157	-107	Updated estimate
Capital and Other Costs				
Amortized (7-year)	714	875	-161	Updated estimate
Utilities, rent		57	-57	Not estimated in Phase 2
Profit	1094	1028	66	Updated estimate

53

(Solmat3.to1)

7.0 HELIOSTAT TESTING

In the following sections the results of heliostat canting, structural tests, optical tests, controls tests, and reliability data are presented.

7.1   Heliostat Canting

Heliostat facet canting measurements made on the Sandia heliostat were analyzed. The measurements were taken before the heliostat was re-aligned to remove the divergence of the beams from the left and right halves of the heliostat, and before one facet was moved up into the center of the image. However, the results show a significant variation of the heliostat canting error with elevation angle, and therefore suggest that we have more work to do in the design calculations. Data were taken at 0 degrees, 30 degrees, 60 degrees, 90 degrees, and 115 degrees of heliostat elevation.

The analyses performed on the data at each elevation angle are as follows:

1 .   The canting raw data are entered into a spreadsheet as the z-values for the facet mounting points.
2.   The mounting point x and y values are taken off the AutoCAD assembly drawing of the heliostat.
3.   The x,y,z triples for each facet are used to determine the location of the center of each facet and the orientation of the facet normal.
4.   The x,y center location of the facet is used to determine the orientation of the normal vector for a paraboloid of revolution of the focal length of the heliostat.
5.   The normals to the facet and the paraboloid are compared to determine the angle between them, giving the individual facet canting errors.
6.   X and Y offsets are determined which minimize the canting errors. This takes out any pointing errors relative to the heliostat centerline.
7.   The individual canting errors are averaged to obtain the heliostat overall canting error.

In order to illustrate the canting errors, the facet normals were projected to a plane at twice the focal length. This gives a picture of what the reflected images at the focal length would look like.

The results of the analysis are presented in the attached pictures. **Figure 7-1** shows the average and maximum canting errors as a function of the elevation angle of the heliostat. The following graphs (**Figures 7-2** through **7-6**) show the images of each facet projected to twice the focal length. Note that the x-axis is positive to the East, so the images are as if one were looking at the back of a target, towards the front of the heliostat. The y-axis is positive upward.

54

Figure 7-1. Average and Maximum Canting Errors

Sandia Heliostat Canting Test Results

Elevation	Avg. Error	Max. Error
0	4.89	8.45
30	2.68	8.46
60	1.31	5.26
90	1.43	5.27
115	1.76	4.93

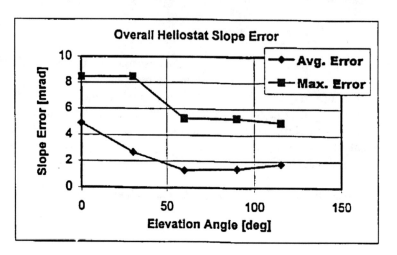

Figure 7-2. Images of Each Facet at Zero Degrees Elevation

Sandia Heliostat Canting Test Results

Zero Degrees Elevation

260 meter focal length

Mounting locations taken from H2-0000

4.89 mrad average slope error

8.45 mrad max error

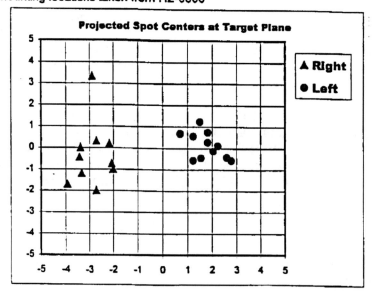

(Solmat3.to1)

Figure 7-3. Images of Each Facet at 30 Degree Elevation

Sandia Heliostat Canting Test Results

30 Degree Elevation   2.68 mrad average slope error

   260 meter focal length   8.46 mrad max error

Mounting locations taken from H2-0000

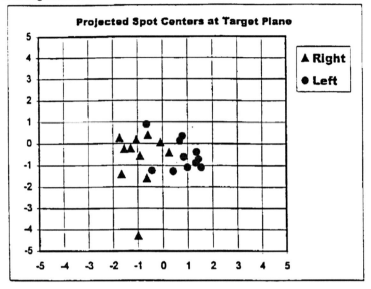

Figure 7-4. Images of Each Facet at 60 Degrees Elevation

Sandia Heliostat Canting Test Results

60 Degree Elevation   1.31 mrad average slope error

   260 meter focal length   5.26 mrad max error

Mounting locations taken from H2-0000

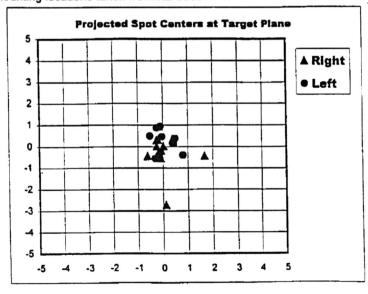

(Solmat3.to1)

Figure 7-5. Images of Each Facet at 90 Degree Elevation

Sandia Heliostat Canting Test Results

90 Degree Elevation   1.43 mrad average slope error

   260 meter focal length   5.27   mrad max error

Mounting locations taken from H2-0000

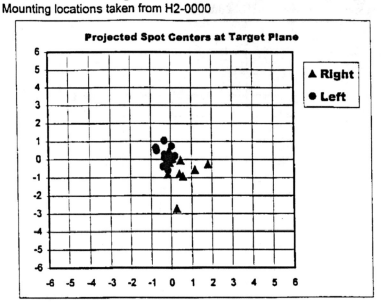

Figure 7-6. Images of Each Facet at 115 Degrees Elevation

Sandia Heliostat Canting Test Results

115 Degree Elevation   1.76 mrad average slope error

   260 meter focal length   4.93   mrad max error

Mounting locations taken from H2-0000

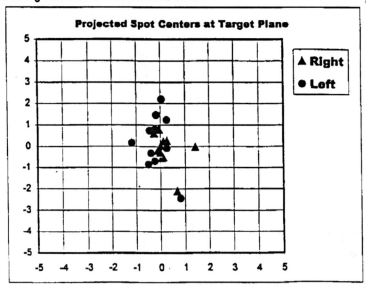

57

7.2   Structural Deflection Tests

Deflection tests to measure the structural deflection of the torque tube and facet mounting points versus elevation angle were accomplished to determine the effect of gravity on the structure. As indicated earlier, the torque tubes on the Golden heliostat were initially found to have excessive sag. The sag was reduced on the Golden unit by welding ribs to the torque tube perimeter near the drive where the highest bending moments occur. Diagonal struts were also added from the tip of each truss to the top-center of the heliostat. The resulting deflection of the torque tube vs elevation angle is shown in **Figure 7-7.** The stiffening effect of the ribs near the drive is evident. Also the major effect the diagonal struts have in limiting tip deflection at low elevation angles is shown, as compared to the minimal effect the struts have at high elevation angles.

For the subsequent heliostats in Albuquerque and Barstow, the torque tube diameter was increase from 18 in. to 24 in. As shown in **Figure 7-8,** the stiffer torque tubes made a large difference in minimizing torque tube deflection. The pointing errors for each heliostat were also determined from the facet mounting point deflections. As shown in **Figure 7-9,** larger torque tube helped dramatically in limiting pointing errors.

7.3 Optical Image Tests

7.3.1   Off-Axis Image

As analysis was performed of the image shapes one should expect from the heliostat at Sandia compared to the BCS images recorded at Sandia. The results indicate that heliostat behaves as expected, and the distortions of the images that have been observed are due primarily to geometric effects of the incidence angle of the sun and the heliostats position relative to the tower.

Basically, two independent mirrors (left and right of the drive) were assumed, with a fixed cant angle between them. Then, the effort looked at what would happen to the resulting image on the target as you changed the azimuth incidence angle of the sun to the heliostat. In the limit of an angle of incidence of zero (sun on the heliostat axis), the canting angles to place both images at the same point was set. For the 254.7m distance from the Sandia heliostat to the BCS target, the resulting angle is .010 radians on each side (one positive, one negative). In the other limit of glancing incidence on one of the mirrors, the resulting reflection from the other mirror would be displaced by four times the canting angle (i.e., 2x due to reflection, and 2x because the total angle between the mirrors is twice the canting angle). Thus, at that limit, the images would be displaced by 0.040 radians. At a range of 254.7m, the images from the two halves of the heliostat would be displaced approximately 10.2 meters from one another. Of course, at glancing incidence, the images would also be very much foreshortened in the azimuth direction. If originally circular, they would become elliptical with the same height but a much-reduced width.

58

Figure 7-7. Golden Heliostat — Torque Tube Sag at Various Elevation Angles

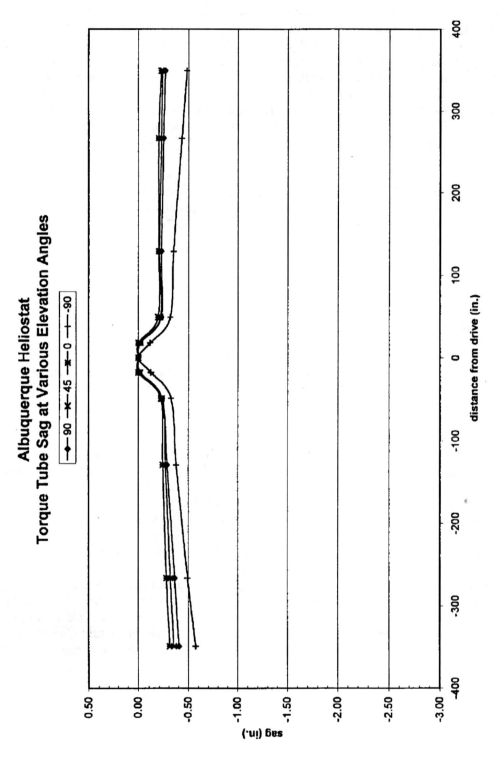

Albuquerque Heliostat
Torque Tube Sag at Various Elevation Angles

SolMat

Printed: 9/14/98

Albuquerque Heliostat Truss and Torque Tube Deformations a.xls

(Solmat3.to1)

Figure 7-8. Albuquerque Heliostat — Torque Tube Sag at Various Elevation Angles

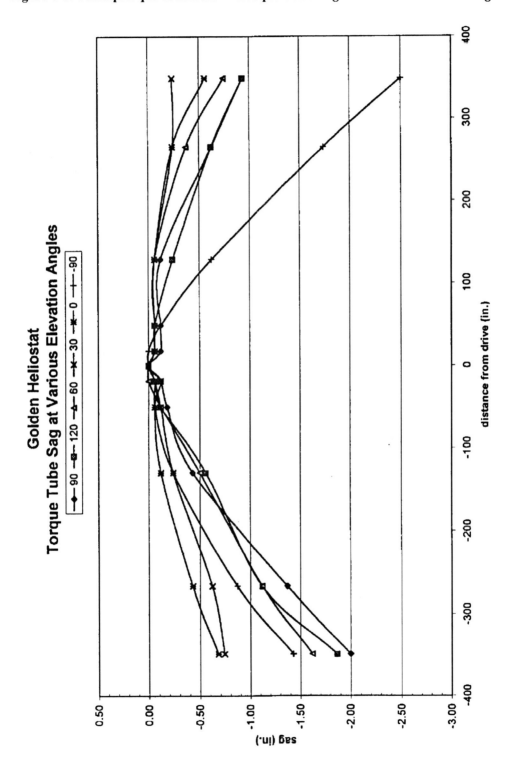

Printed: 9/14/98

NREL Heliostat Truss and Torque Tube Deformations.xls

(Solmat3.to1)

Figure 7-9. Average Facet Pointing Errors (referenced from 60 degrees of elevation)

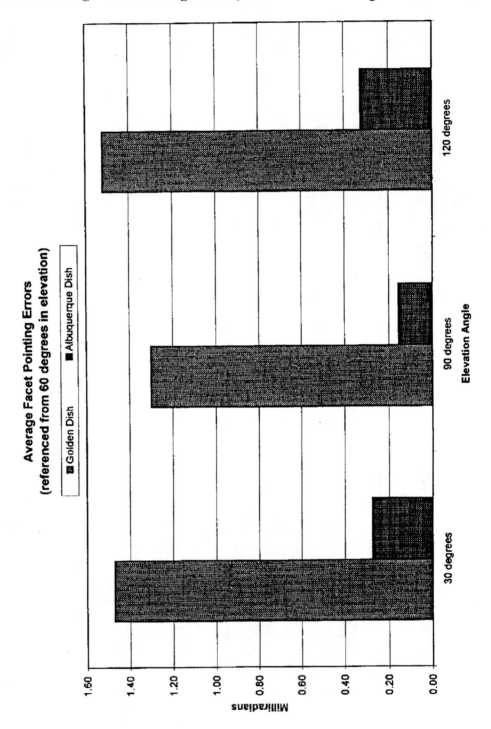

61

Between the two limits described above, the behavior of the two images is more complex, but generally the separation between the images increases monotonically as the incidence angle increases. A simple analysis to determine the functional relationship between the image displacement and the incidence angle was performed, with the results shown on **Figure 7-10.** The table at the upper right includes the incidence angle (in degrees), the displacement between the two images (in meters) and the image widths for each of the two mirrors, assuming an initial mirror image width of 3.2 in. The graph plots the displacement as a function of the incidence angle. As shown, the displacement of the images is less than their radii (so they would overlap) up to about 30 degrees angle of incidence, and increases from there to a displacement of over 10 in near 90 degrees angle of incidence.

Next, some tracking results for the Sandia heliostat were used to generate azimuth incidence angles as a function of time. **Figure 7-11** shows the data, which was from 3/3/98. The azimuth incidence angles were then used to estimate the expected horizontal displacement of the images from the heliostat as a function of time. **Figure 7-12** shows the results. The estimated horizontal displacements are shown on the graph as the line with the filled squares as a marker symbol.

Finally, the BCS images measured at Sandia were used to measure actual displacements between the images over the course of a day of tracking. The only data available are shown in **Figure 7-13.** The images are identified by the Julian Day (007) and the time (e.g., 0741) of the image. The data was taken 1/7/98. Estimating the circular diameter of the images as 4 meters, the horizontal displacements for each time by direct measurement were estimated. Then the displacements as a function of time were plotted. The results are shown on **Figure 7-12,** as the line identified by the filled diamonds.

Figure-7-10. Azimuth Incidence Angles

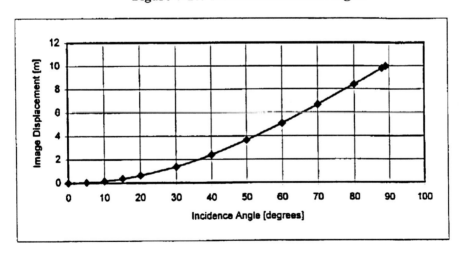

(Solmat3.to1)

Figure 7-11. Horizontal Displacement-Function of Time

Sandia Heliostat Tracking Results – 3 March 1998

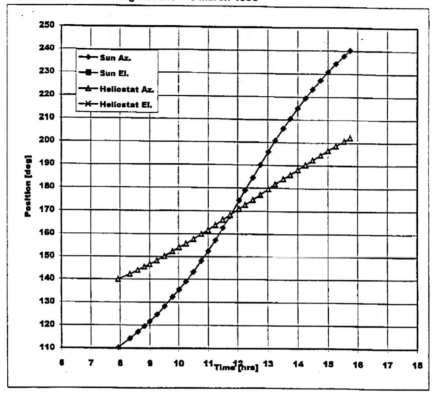

Figure 7-12. Horizontal Displacement of Heliostat Images

Time	Estimated from 3/3/98 Data	Measured 1/7/98
7.75	1.36	2
8.2	1.27	1.8
8.75	1.03	1.4
9.75	0.6	0.5
10.25	0.5	0.2
10.75	0.19	0
11.2	0.125	0
11.5	0.025	-0.2
11.75	0	-0.4
12.2	-0.076	-0.4
12.7	-0.26	-0.4
13.2	-0.55	-0.4
13.7	-0.95	-0.4
14.2	-1.36	-0.4
14.7	-1.64	-1
15.2	-2.05	-1.5
15.7	-2.15	-2
16.2	-2.61	-2.5
16.6	-3.1	-3

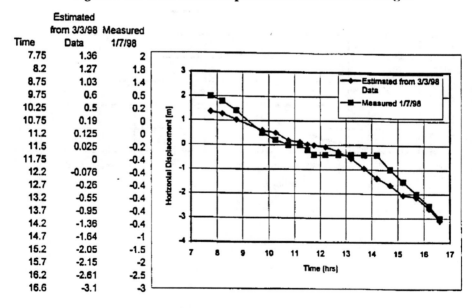

63

Despite the difference of about two months between the data sets, the agreement between these rough estimates is very good. Both the magnitude and the trend of the displacements match to well within the errors of the estimates. Thus, the image displacements seen in the BCS images would appear to be explainable by the canting geometry of the two mirror halves of the heliostat and the sun incidence angle.

The vertical displacements between the two halves of the heliostat image shown on the BCS images are due to the change in the orientation of the heliostat relative to the tower over the course of the day. When one half of the heliostat is closer to the tower, the image from that half appears lower on the target than the other image because it is intercepted by the tower sooner as it rises from the heliostat. The effort didn't analyze this effect, but the effect is clear from an intuitive perspective.

7.3.2 Sandia Optical Tests

The heliostat at the NSTTF, Sandia National Laboratories was extensively tested using a Beam Characterization System (BCS). BCS data for three days in the Winter (1/7/98), Spring (3/19/98), and Summer (6/1/98) is shown in **Figures 7-13 through 7-15.** The heliostat was canted in Winter, therefore the spreading of the image due to off-axis abberation is smallest at this time of year. As shown, the worst off-axis abberation occurs at low elevation angles in the Summer. The pronounced abberation at low heliostat incident angles is due to the short slant range to the receiver, and large size of the heliostat.

Several other types of data plots for these three days are shown on the following figures. **Figures 7-16 through 7-20** show the cosine effect, solar insolation, total beam power, peak flux, and effective beam diameter versus time for 3/19/98. **Figures 7-21 and 7-22** show the movement of the beam centroid on the target with time. **Figure 7-23** shows the wind speed during the test. Comparable data for Summer (6/1/98) is shown on **Figures 7-24 through 7-31.** Less data is available for 1/7/98. The effective beam diameter, beam centroid movement, and wind speed are shown on **Figures 7-32 through 7-35.**

7.4 Control System Tests

The SolMaT heliostat controller hardware and software have been under test since March 1997. The first release of the complete software package was on 28 March 1997.

A brassboard system was developed and connected to a spare drive unit at the SAIC office in March 1997. On 22-27 March, repeatability tests were conducted on the limit switches. The system was manually driven onto the limit switches and the azimuth and elevation motor counts were recorded. On 31 March, the system was commanded to track the computed sun position, and the difference between the commanded and reported position was recorded. Over an eight hour period, the average deviations from the commanded positions were 0.018 degrees in azimuth and 0.002 degrees in elevation, with no apparent drift in either axis. On 9 May, new limit switches were installed, and the system was repeatedly driven onto the elevation switch to

(Solmat3.to1)

Figure 7-13. SAIC SolMaT Heliostat on 1/7/98 (007), 174.1 sqm, 10 % isocontour lines of peak intensity, 5 m diameter circle at centroid

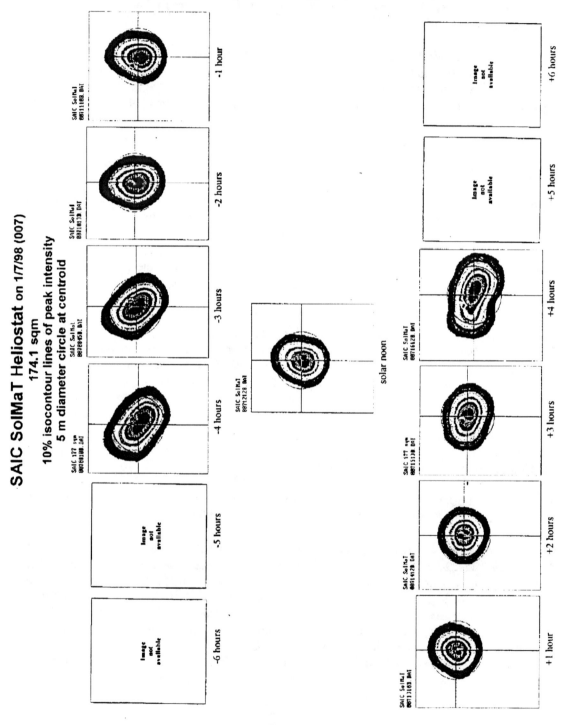

(Solmat3.to1)

Figure 7-14. SAIC SolMaT Heliostat on 3/19/98 (day 78), 174.1 sqm, 10 % isocontour lines of peak intensity, 5 m diameter circle at centroid

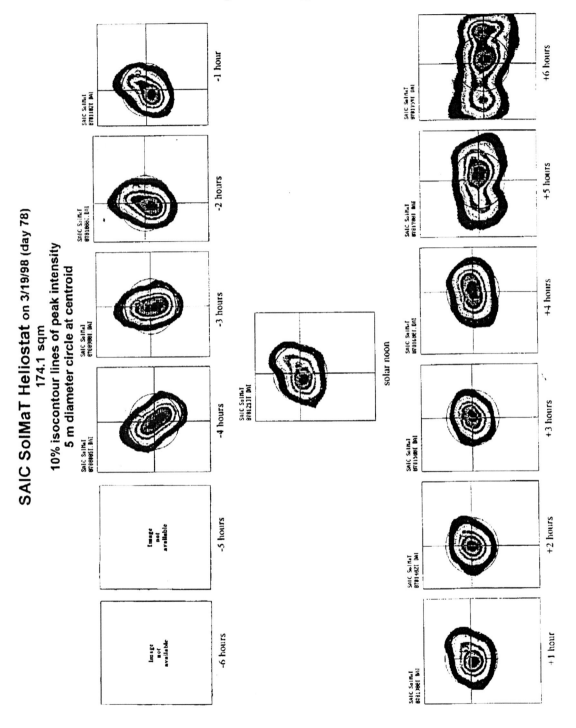

Figure 7-15. SAIC SolMaT Heliostat on 6/1-4/98 (152-4), 174.1 sqm, 10 % isocontour lines of peak intensity, 5 m diameter circle at centroid

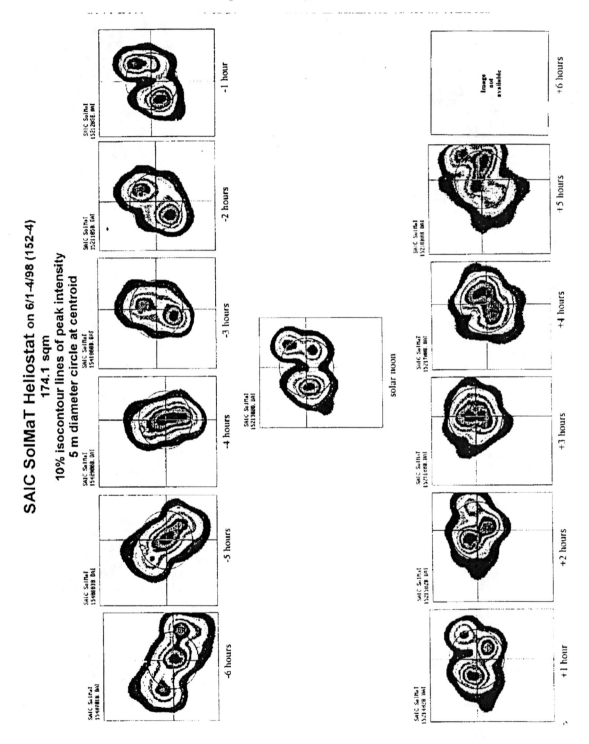

67

Figure 7-16. SAIC on 3/19/98, Cosine Effect

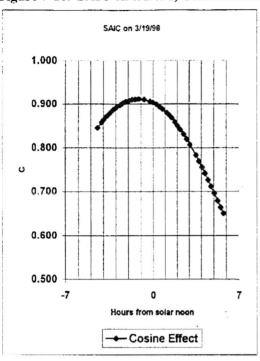

Figure 7-17. SAIC on 3/19/98, NIP

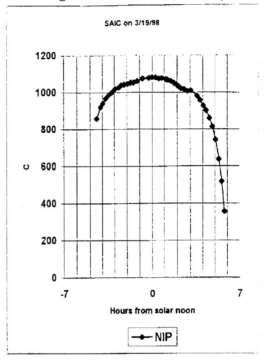

Figure 7-18. SAIC on 3/19/98, Calculated Beam Total Power

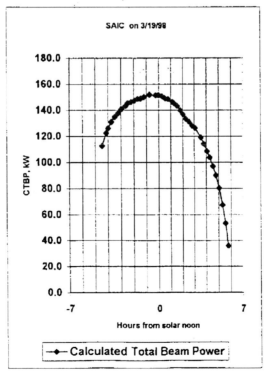

(Solmat3.to1)

Figure 7-19. SAIC on 3/19/98, Peak Flux

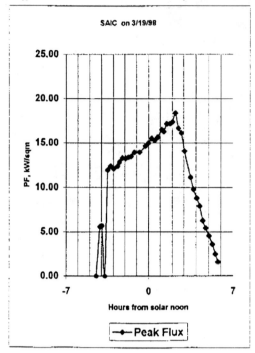

Figure 7-20. SAIC on 3/19/98, Effective Beam Diameter, 90% Beam Power

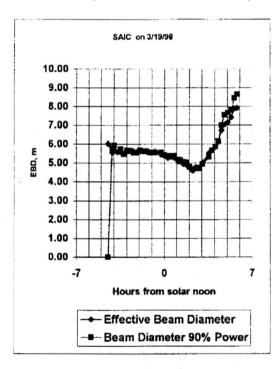

(Solmat3.to1)

Figure 7-21. SAIC on 3/19/98, Average, Minimum and Maximum Centroid

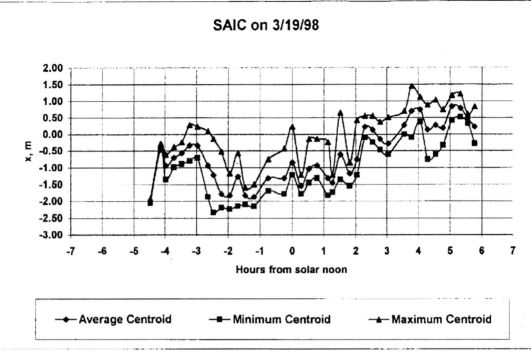

Figure 7-22. SAIC on 3/19/98, Average, Minimum and Maximum x Centroid

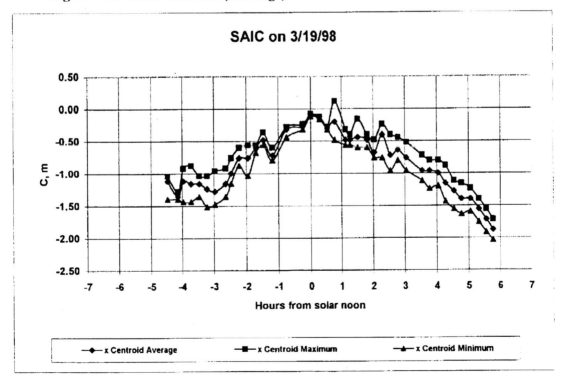

(Solmat3.to1)

Figure 7-23. SAIC on 3/19/98, Wind Speed

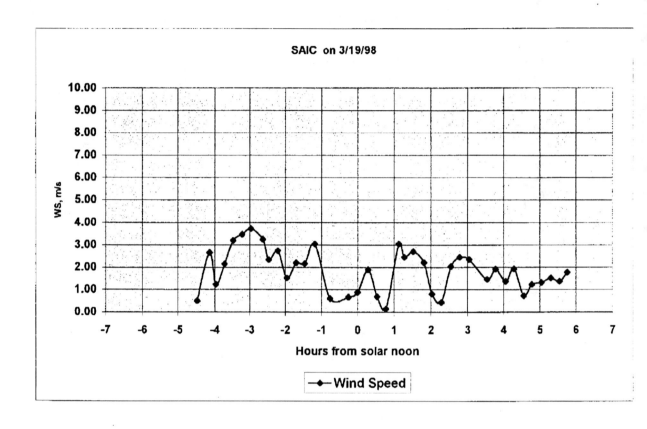

71

Figure 7-24. SAIC on 6/1-3/98, Cosine Effect

Figure 7-25. SAIC on 6/1-3/98, NIP

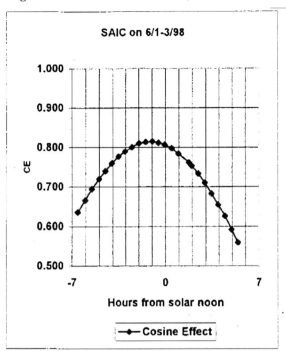

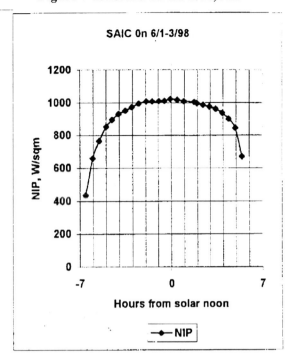

Figure 7-26. SAIC on 6/1-3/98, Calculated Beam Total Power

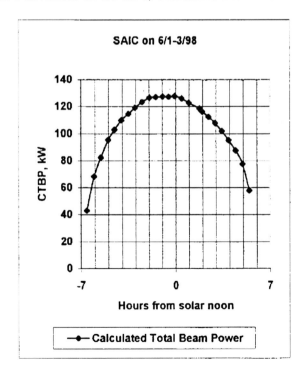

72

Figure 7-27. SAIC on 6/1-3/98, Peak Flux

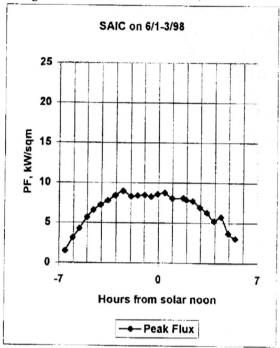

Figure 7-28. SAIC on 6/1-3/98, Effective Beam Diameter, 90% Beam Power

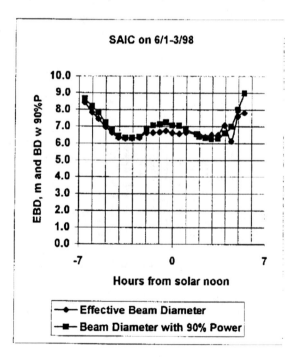

73

Figure 7-29. SAIC on 6/1-3/98, Average, Minimum and Maximum x Centroid

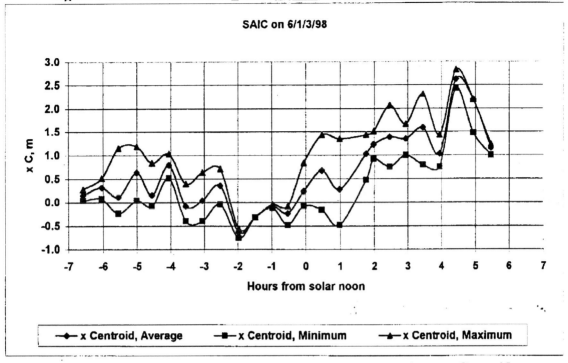

Figure 7-30. SAIC on 6/1-3/98, Average, Minimum and Maximum y Centroid

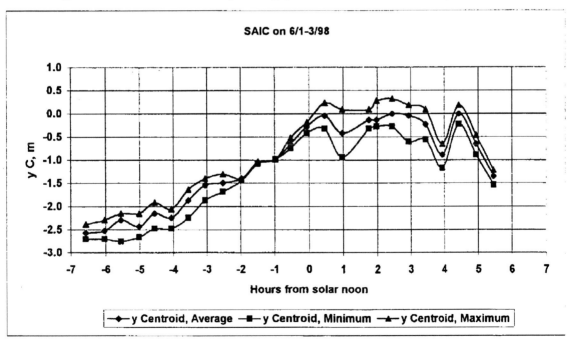

(Solmat3.to1)

Figure 7-31. SAIC on 6/1-3/98, Wind Speed

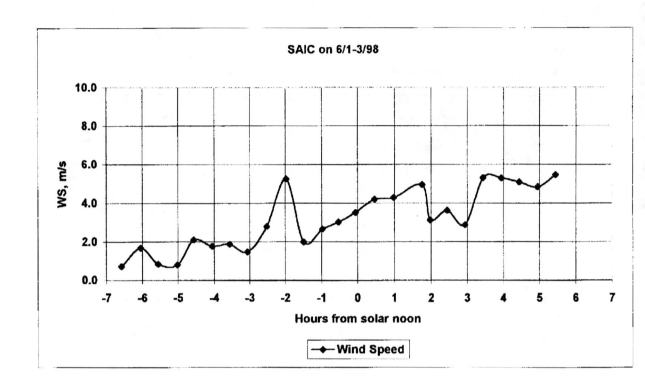

75

Figure 7-32. SAIC on 1/7/98, Effective Beam Diameter, Circle Diameter 90% Power

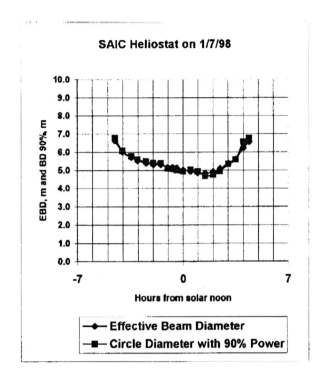

Figure 7-33. SAIC on 1/7/98, x Centroid

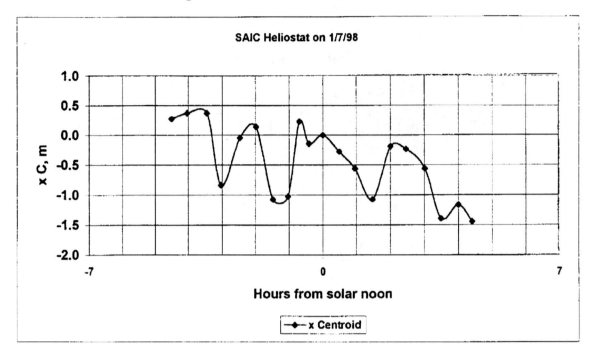

Figure 7-34. SAIC on 1/7/98, y Centroid

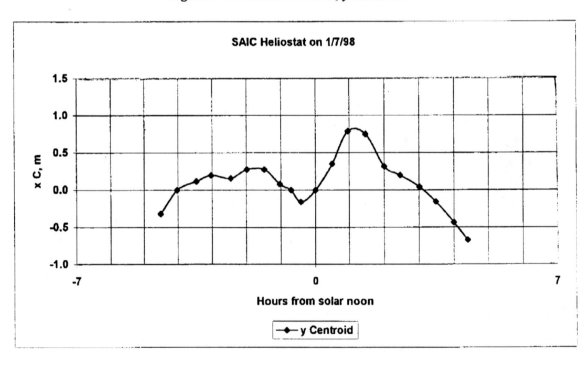

(Solmat3.to1)

Figure 7-35. SAIC on 1/7/98, Wind Speed m/s, Wind Speed mph

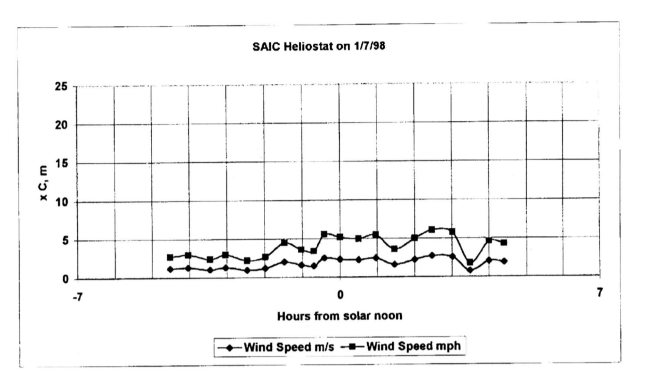

(Solmat3.to1)

Figure 7-36. Brassboard System

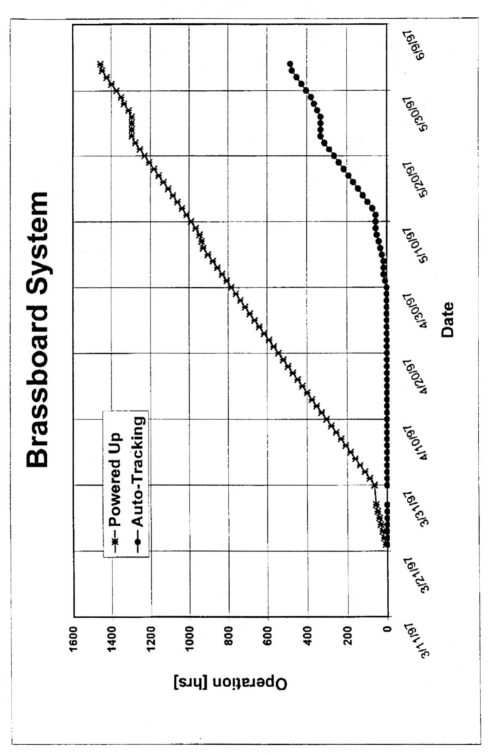

check its repeatability. The results were that the value remained constant over 10 trials with a standard deviation of only 0.006 degrees.

Beginning on 31 March, the brassboard system was powered up and commanded to track the sun. Beginning on 12 May, the system was developed to the point where it was left in automatic tracking mode overnight. **Figure 7-37** shows that 1,455 cumulative hours of powered-up operation and 482 hours of automatic tracking were accumulated through 3 June, when the first heliostat controller board was substituted for the brassboard and began testing.

Figure 7-38 documents the bench testing performed on the first heliostat control board. Testing began on 3 June, and except for a few days in which the control computer was taken away for other tasks, the system operated in an automatic tracking mode until it was moved to the heliostat in July. Through 21 July, the system accumulated 1153 hours of powered-up operation, and 1021 hours of automated tracking operation. A log of system anomalies was kept during the test. Most of the errors were related to communications between the heliostat controller and the PC host computer. These were resolved through changes made to the PC host software. The fuse blown on 13 July was the first hardware failure except for an incorrectly wired encoder detected early in the testing. There was no apparent cause for the failure of the fuse, but since both motors are rated at 7 Amps full-load, it may have been a case where both motors started at once and caused a longer-than-usual peak load. It did not repeat, and larger fuses were used in the heliostat installations.

(Solmat3.to1)

Figure 7-37 Heliostat Controller #1

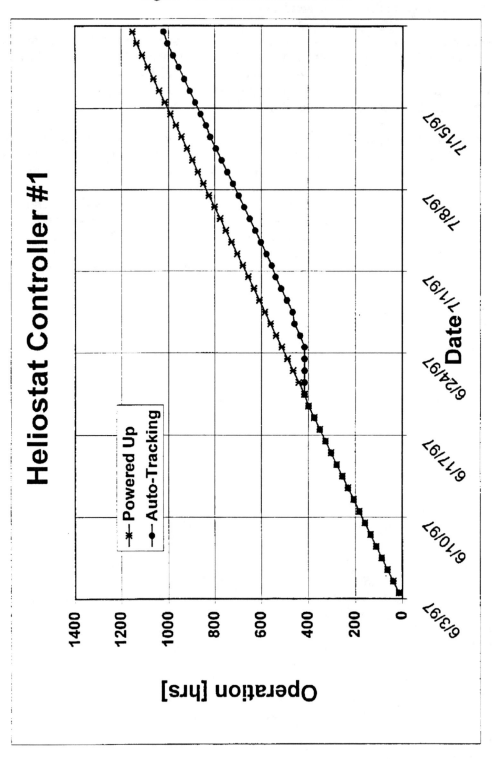

81

Tracking tests were also performed in that period. **Figure 7-38** shows the results of a bench-test of tracking conducted over a 5.5-hour period. During that time, the average error was about 0.02 degrees from the desired aim point, with a 0.02-degree standard deviation.

Once the heliostats were installed, tests were conducted to verify their correct operation. **Figure 7-39** shows the result of the tilt correction test performed on the NREL heliostat. As shown in the figure, the tilt correction reduced the average azimuth error from 0.06 degrees to 0.00 degrees, with a standard deviation of 0.03 degrees. The elevation error was decreased from 0.21 degrees to 0.00 degrees with a standard deviation of 0.04 degrees.

Finally, the systems were operated in an automated manner to accumulate operating hours on the control system and structure. **Figures 7-40** and **7-41** show the monthly and cumulative hours of operation for the NREL and Sandia heliostats through June 1998. The NREL heliostat, which has been in operation since August 1997, has accumulated over 6,500 hours of powered-up time, and has operated 882 hours in automatic tracking mode. The Sandia heliostat has over 5,200 hours of powered-up time and has operated over 1200 hours in automatic tracking mode.

7.5 Reliability Data

Both of the heliostats installed at NREL and Sandia have been studied for their reliability. **Figures 7-42** and **7-43** show the monthly availability and utilization for the two systems from the time of their installations through June 1998. As shown in the figures, the heliostats have had very high availability's of well over 90%.

Tables 7-15 and **7-16** show reliability summaries for the NREL and Sandia systems respectively. They include Mean-Time-Between Failures, Mean-Time-To-Repair, and probability of failure free operation calculation.

7.6 High Wind Stow and Reflectance Data

The number of automatic stows due to high wind by month for both the Golden and Albuquerque are shown in **Figures 7-44 and 7-45.** The number of high wind stows is effected by both the wind speed and the amount of time the heliostat was tracking during the month.

Reflectance of the heliostat facets was measured at both sites. The measurements showed an RMS average reflectance of 89.1 % with a standard deviation of 0.5 at both sites.

(Solmat3.to1)

Figure 7-38. Results of Bench-Test Tracking

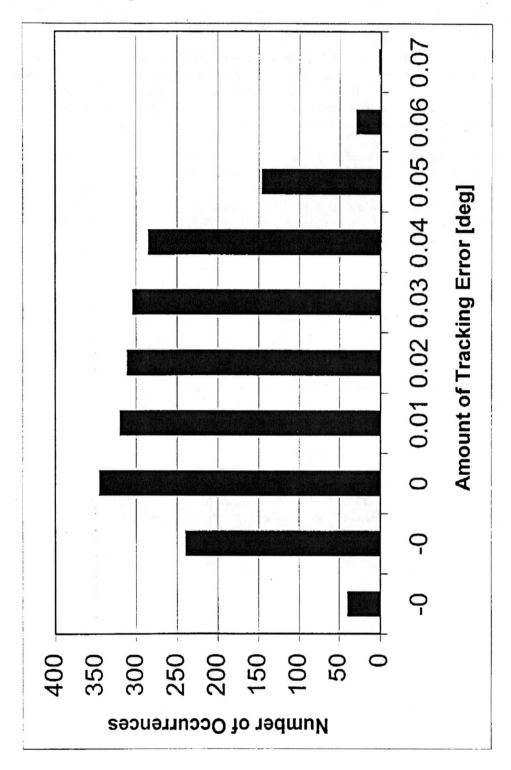

83

(Solmat3.to1)

Figure 7-39. Results of Tilt Correction

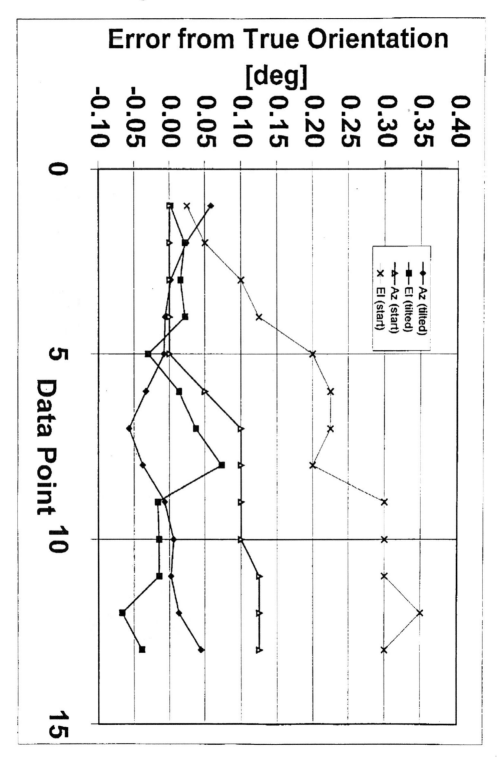

(Solmat3.to1)

Figure 7-40. Monthly and Cumulative Hours of Operation – Golden Heliostat

SolMat Golden Heliostat Performance Summary

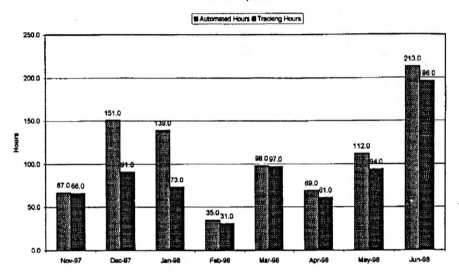

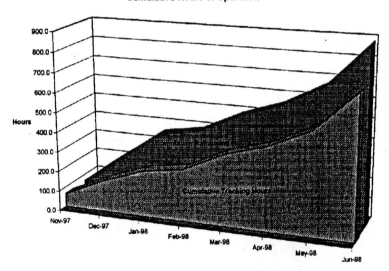

Overall Performance for the Golden Heliostat.xls   Printed 8/5/98

85

(Solmat3.to1)

Figure 7-41. Monthly and Cumulative Hours of Operation – Albuquerque Heliostat

SolMat Albuquerque Heliostat Performance Summary

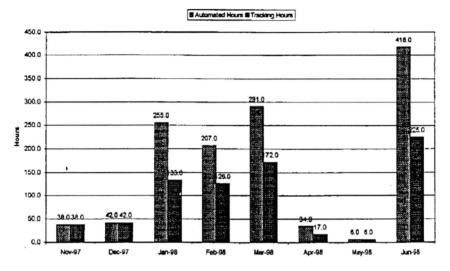

Albuquerque Heliostat
Hours of Operation

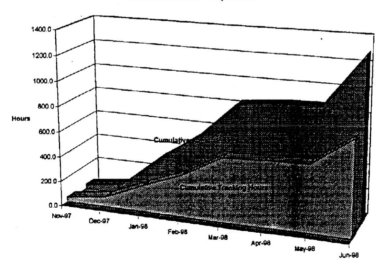

Albuquerque Heliostat
Cumulative Hours of Operation

Figure 7-42. Golden Heliostat – Availability and Utilization

SolMat Golden Heliostat Performance Summary

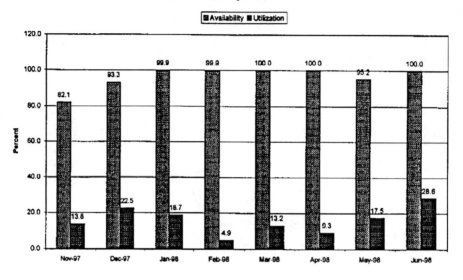

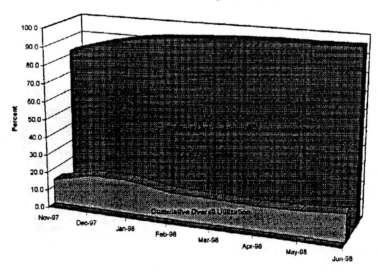

Overall Performance for the Golden Heliostat.xls

Printed 8/5/98

87

(Solmat3.to1)

Figure 7-43. Albuquerque Heliostat – Availability and Utilization

SolMat Albuquerque Heliostat Performance Summary

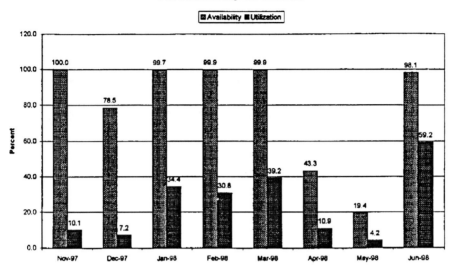

Albuquerque Heliostat
Overall Availability and Utilization

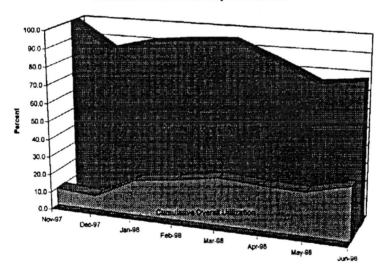

Albuquerque Heliostat
Cumulative Overall Availability and Utilization

Overall Performance for the Albuquerque Heliostat.xls   Printed 8/5/98

(Solmat3.to1)

Figure 7-44. Reliability Summary – NREL Heliostat

SolMat Golden Heliostat Performance Summary

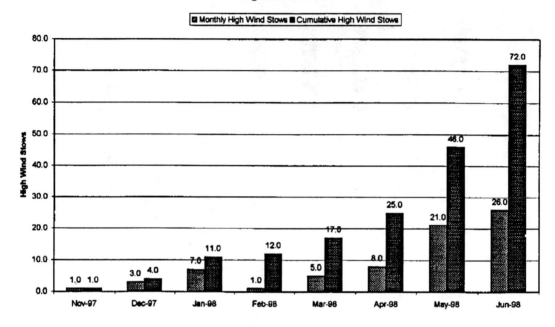

Golden Heliostat
High Wind Stows

(Solmat3.to1)

Figure 7-45. Reliability Summary – Sandia Heliostat

SolMat Albuquerque Heliostat Performance Summary

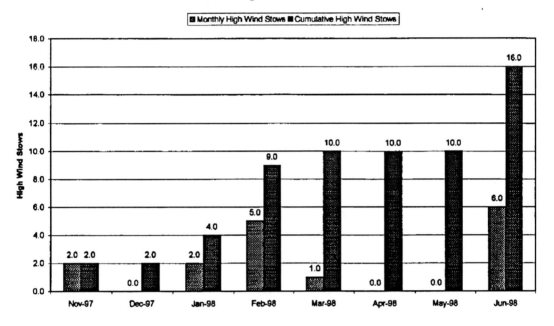

Albuquerque Heliostat
High Wind Stows

☒ Monthly High Wind Stows ■ Cumulative High Wind Stows

90

8.0 MARKET ASSESSMENT

The following subsections give a market assessment for production and sales of heliostats. This assessment was originally developed in Phase I of this program. The first subsections describe the market environment for solar central receives power plants into which the SAIC heliostat will be marketed and the technologies for power plants and heliostats. Following that is an analysis that compares the allowable cost of a heliostat to the requirements of the marketplace, and suggests a market entry and business development strategy. Next, a market analysis with possible medium, and long-term markets is presented, including descriptions of specific market opportunities.

Then, a commercial production approach for heliostats to meet the market needs is detailed. Finally, an evaluation of competing products and technologies is presented, and barriers to market entry are evaluated.

8.1   Technology Description

The principal design and performance characteristics of a central receiver power plant, and the heliostats in the collector system are outlined in the following sections.

8. 1. 1. Central Receiver Power Plant
The principal types of central receiver power plants are the solar-only Rankine cycle power plant and the hybrid fossil-solar combined cycle power plant.

Solar-Only Rankine Cycle Power Plant
The central receiver concept uses an array of large, moveable mirrors (heliostats) to redirect and concentrate sunlight on a receiver located at the top of a tower. The concentrated flux on the receiver heats a liquid nitrate salt from an inlet temperature of 550°F to an outlet temperature of 1,050°F. The nitrate salt is stored in a high temperature thermal storage tank then withdrawn from the tank and delivered to a steam generator. The nitrate salt cools from a steam generator inlet temperature of 1,050°F to an outlet temperature of 5,500°F. The low temperature nitrate salt is stored in a cold thermal storage tank, then withdrawn from the tank to supply the receiver and complete the cycle. Thermal energy transferred in the steam generator generates superheated main and reheat steam at a temperature of 1,000°F. Energy in the steam is converted to electric energy in a conventional Rankine cycle power plant. A schematic process diagram is shown in **Figure 8-1.**

The plant consists of two independent loops: one for collecting thermal energy and the second for converting thermal energy to electric energy. Thermal energy is collected in the following systems:

- Collector system, which concentrates direct normal radiation on the receiver. The principal equipment are the heliostats, heliostat controllers, and field wiring.

- Receiver system, which converts the concentrated radiation into heat and transfers the energy to the nitrate salt coolant. The principal equipment are the receiver, tower, cold nitrate salt pumps, cold nitrate salt pump sump, riser piping, and downcomer piping.

Figure 8-1. Solar-Only Central Receiver Plant

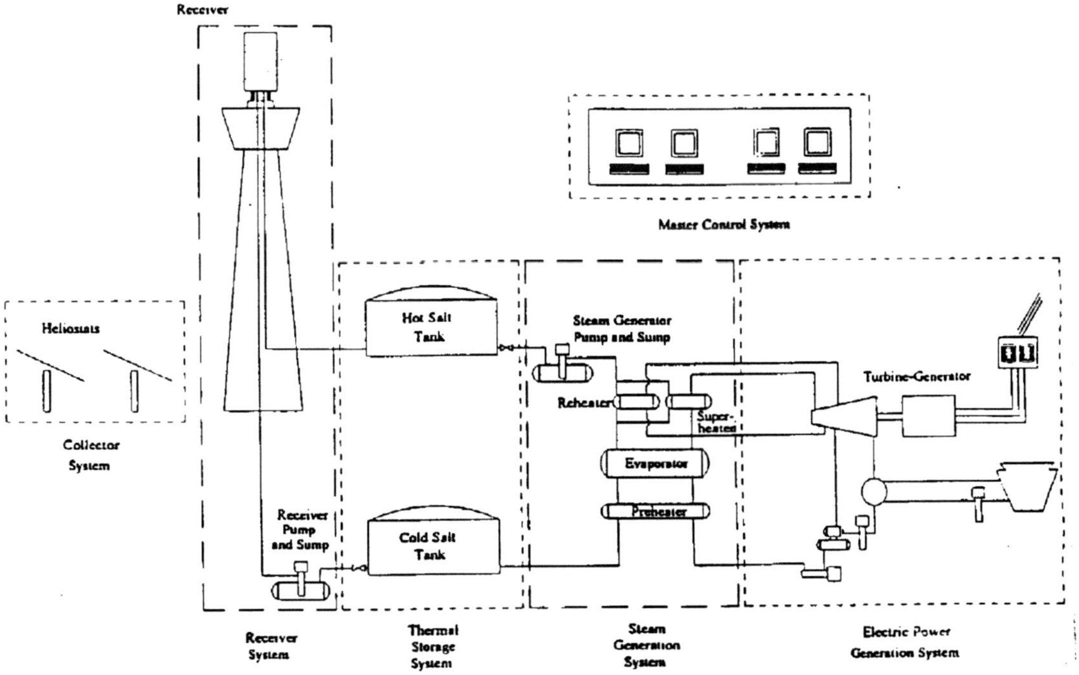

- Thermal storage system which stores high and low temperature nitrate salt for use in the steam generation and receiver systems, respectively. The system isolates the turbine generator from short-term variations in the direct normal radiation, and provides a source of energy for operating the turbine-generator late in the afternoon or early in the evening. The principal equipment are the cold and hot thermal storage tanks, and the nitrate salt inventory.

The thermal energy is converted to electric energy in the following systems:

- Steam generation system, which transfers energy from the nitrate salt to the feedwater to produce superheated steam. The major equipment are the nitrate salt-to-water or nitrate salt to-steam heat exchangers (superheater, reheater, evaporator, and preheater), hot nitrate salt pumps, cold nitrate salt mixer pump, and the hot nitrate salt pump sump.

- Electric power generation system, which converts the energy in the superheated steam into electric energy. The principal equipment are the turbine-generator and balance of plant systems.

92

The master control system controls the operation of all the plant systems. The major equipment items are the distributed process control system, programmable logic controller, data acquisition system, and software,

Hybrid Fossil Fuel-Solar Central Receiver Power Plant

A variation on the solar-only plant is a hybrid fossil energy/solar energy central receiver concept. Thermal energy from the central receiver plant is introduced in a combined cycle plant at the following two locations:

- Compressed air stream between the gas turbine compressor outlet and the combustor inlet. This preheats the combustion air stream and reduces the use of fossil fuel.

- Evaporation section in the heat recovery steam generator. This increases the superheated steam flow to the steam turbine, and increases the annual energy output of the plant.

A schematic diagram of a hybrid combined cycle-central receiver plant is shown in **Figure 8-2.**

Adding a central receiver plant to a commercial combined cycle plant offers several advantages:

- Small- to medium-size central receiver plants can be economically constructed. This minimizes the technical risks in scaling the technology from the 42.6 MW_t receiver of the Solar Two project to the 300 to 400 MW_t receivers of the first commercial solar-only plants.

- Financial risks are minimized because the central receiver plant size can be small and, should the central receiver plant not perform as expected, the annual plant output can remain high.

(Solmat3.to1)

Figure 8-2. Combined-Cycle-Central Receiver Power Plant

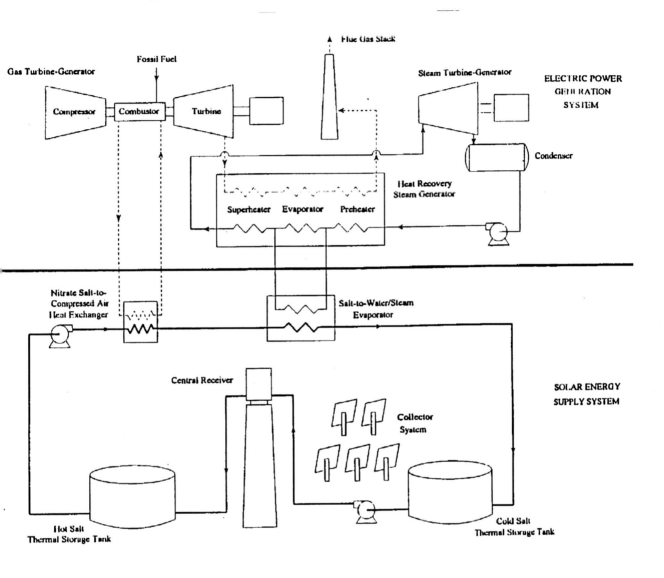

(Solmat3.to1)

- Solar energy contributions to the annual energy production use can range from 5 to 60 percent. Thus, the design, performance and economics of the central receiver plant can readily be tailored to meet the requirements of the site or the local utility. With inexpensive fossil fuel prices, plants with low solar fractions will be the option of choice.

- The efficiency of a combined cycle plant is greater than a reheat Rankine cycle plant, Thus, the energy supplied by a central receiver plant to a combined cycle plant is used more efficiently than if supplied to a Rankine cycle plant.

8.1.2. Heliostats
The collector system consists of the following items:

- Glass/metal or stretched membrane heliostats.

- Heliostat controller hardware and software.

- Field power, control, and ground wiring.

The size of the collector system is a function of the plant size and the desired capacity factor. For example, a collector system for 100 MW_e, (net) plant sized to meet only the thermal demand of the steam generator at noon on the summer solstice might require 500,000 m^2 of reflector area and deliver 300 MWt to the receiver. In contrast, a collector system for the same turbine plant sized for an annual capacity factor of 60 percent might require 1,400,000 m^2 and deliver 850 MW, to the receiver. The selection of the optimum reflector area is a function of the values of energy and capacity to the local utility.

Heliostat Field Layout
A typical commercial plant design employs a single, cylindrical receiver with a collector field surrounding the tower. The receiver geometry (absorber height and diameter) tower height, and heliostat locations are determined by the RCELL group of computer programs. The program develops a degraded image of the sun formed by partially focused heliostats aimed at the receiver surface. The projection, modeled using Hermite polynomials, is determined for a representative heliostat in each of several cells, which comprise the heliostat field. For each representative heliostat, the annual effects of shading, blocking, and cosine losses are calculated over a range of spacings to the nearest neighbors. The resulting database is interrogated by an optimization processor to determine the azimuthal and radial spacing to neighbors, which produces the same normalized performance everywhere in the field.

The program models the following items to select the design, which offers the lowest annual cost of thermal energy at the base of the tower:

- Annual clear sky directs beam radiation, modified by the effects of cloud cover and atmospheric turbidity.

95

- Peak flux limits, consistent with the local nitrate salt bulk temperatures.

- Capital costs, and present value of operation and maintenance, for the following:
  - land
  - heliostats
  - field power, control, and ground wiring
  - tower, as a function of height
  - receiver, as a function of absorber area
  - cold nitrate salt pumps, as a function of flow rate and pressure drop
  - riser and downcomer piping, as a function of flow rate and tower height.

- Equivalent capital costs for the annual electric energy use of the following:
  - heliostat drive motor and focus control mechanisms
  - cold nitrate salt pumps.

Outputs from the program include the following:

- Optimum heliostat locations, receiver dimensions, and tower height.

- Field efficiency matrix, showing the composite heliostat field optical efficiency on 8 days during the year (I day for each month from the winter solstice to the summer solstice) and 7 equally-spaced times from sunrise to noon on the selected days. Sun position symmetry over the course of a year and the course of a day, and bicubic spline interpolations within the table, allow the performance of the field to be estimated at any time of the day on any day of the year.

- Incident receiver flux maps for representative times throughout the year.

8.2   Business Hypothesis

8.2. 1. Electric Power Market Evolution
The utility industry and the electric supply market have undergone significant change in the past five years. Regulatory reform in wholesale power markets has enhanced the efficiency of inter regional energy transactions, putting downward pressure on prices and reducing new capacity needs. Natural gas supplies appear robust and expectations of price escalation are modest well into the next century. Emerging futures markets in both electric energy and natural gas allow wholesale suppliers to minimize market risk while simultaneously minimizing short-term capital expenditures.

Traditionally, financing and constructing new power plants has been performed by regulated utilities. However, in recent years, the new electric generation market has shifted to finance and construction by independent power producers with energy sales to the utilities. The utilities, in turn, become responsible for power transmission and distribution.

96

The estimated levelized costs of electric energy, in current year dollars, for the principal technologies that will compete in the bulk power markets over the next two decades are shown in Table 8-1.

Table 8-1. Levelized Cost of Electric Energy from Various Technologies, $/kWh$_e$

Technology	Levelized Cost of Electric Energy, $/kWh$_e$	Comments
Wind	0.03 to 0.06	The cost of energy depends on average annual wind speed and the efficiency of the turbine.
Combined Cycle	0.03 to 0.05	The cost of energy is based on natural gas as the fuel source, and is also a function of the plat size and complexity of the heat recovery steam generator.
Combined Cycle	0.04 to 0.07	The cost of energy is based on naphtha or distillate oil as the fuel source, and is also a function of the plant size and complexity of the heat recovery steam generator.
Coal	0.04 to 0.07	The cost of energy is a function of the delivered coal price and the extent of emissions controls.
Hydroelectric	0.06 to 0.12	The cost of energy depends on the reservoir elevation, annual water flow rate, and siting issues.
Biomass	0.06 to 0.08	The cost of energy depends on the fuel heating value, transportation charges, and fuel processing requirements prior to combustion.

8.2.2. Central Receiver Market Position

Southern California Edison Company is leading a consortium, consisting of the Department of Energy and several utilities in the Western states, that has successfully retrofitted the 10 MW$_e$, Solar One central receiver pilot plant near Barstow, California, with a nitrate salt receiver, thermal storage, and steam generator technology. In the modified project, called Solar Two, solar energy is collected in sensible heating of the nitrate salt, which is delivered to a hot storage tank. Upon demand, the hot salt is pumped to a steam generator, and the steam produced is used to drive a turbine/generator. The goal of Solar Two is to reduce to manageable levels the technical and financial risks in building the initial commercial central receiver projects.

Until recently, the initial commercial plants following the Solar Two project were envisioned as either solar-only plants, or hybrid fossil-solar plants with solar contributions to the annual energy production of at least 70 percent, financed and owned by a regulated utility. It was well known that the costs of energy from a central receiver project would be higher than the costs from a conventional fossil power plant. However, it was believed that the benefits of fuel diversity, low emissions, and capacity value offered to the ratepayers and the public utility commissions would offset the higher costs, and the project could be included in the utility rate base.

The changing market drivers discussed above require revisions to the original commercialization strategy. In particular, the projects will be financed and operated by independent power producers. As such, the technical risks will need to be held to a minimum to secure the debt portion of the financing and the levelized cost of energy must be competitive if a power purchase agreement is to be secured with the local utility. An analysis of the competitive position of central receiver technology is outlined in the following sections.

8.2.2.1 Levelized Costs of Energy from Central Receiver Power Plants

A series of parametric financial analyses were conducted to evaluate the costs of electric energy from several different central receiver plant concepts under a range of heliostat costs. The results for a 100 MW$_e$, solar-only plant, a 200 MW$_e$ solar-only plant, and a 170 MW$_e$ combined cycle-central receiver plant are presented in **Tables 8-2, 8-3**, and **8-4**, respectively. The input assumptions to the financial analysis are presented in **Table 8-5**. Note that all of the analyses in Sections 2.1, 2.2, and 2.3 are made without special credits or externalities for the central receiver plants.

Table 8-2. Levelized Cost of Energy for a 100 MW, Solar-Only Plant, $/kWh,

Unit Heliostat Price, $m^2	Annual Capacity Factor		
	40 Percent	56 Percent	67 Percent
220	0.153	0.141	0.133
120	0.116	0.103	0.095
90	0.104	0.092	0.084

Table 8-3. Levelized Cost of Energy for a 200 MW, Solar-Only Plant, $/kWh,

Unit Heliostat Price, $m^2	Annual Capacity Factor		
	40 Percent	56 Percent	67 Percent
220	0.139	0.130	0.124
120	0.105	0.092	0.086
90	0.090	0.081	0.075

(Solmat3.to1)

**Table 8-4. Levelized Cost of Energy for a 170 MW,
Combined Cycle-Central Receiver Plant, $/kWh$_e$,**

Unit Heliostat	Annual Capacity Factor		
Price, $m^2	40 Percent	56 Percent	67 Percent
220	0.055	0.059	0.062
120	0.051	0.052	0.052
90	0.050	0.050	0.050

8.2.2.2 Allowable Heliostat Price as a Function of Fossil Fuel Type and Escalation Rate
Parametric analyses were also conducted to determine the allowable heliostat prices such that the
costs of thermal energy from a central receiver facility would be competitive with thermal energy
from fossil fuel sources. For these analyses, the central receiver facility consists of only the
collector, receiver, and thermal storage systems. Comparisons with combined cycle plants using
natural gas are presented in **Table 8-6,** and comparisons with pulverized coal power plants using
medium-Btu coal are shown in **Table 8-7.**

Table 8-5. Inputs to the Financial Analysis of Central Receiver Projects

Debt Fraction	60 percent
Debt Interest Rate	8 percent
Debt Term	20 years
Debt Coverage Ratio	150 percent
Return on Equity	18 percent
Investment Tax Credit on Qualified Equipment	10 percent
Depreciation Term on Qualified Equipment	5 years
Depreciation Term on Non-Qualified Equipment	15 years
Federal and State Income Tax Rate	40.3 percent
Property Tax Rate	0.0 percent
Property Insurance Rate	0.5 percent
General Escalation Rate	3.5 percent
Natural Gas Price Escalation Rate	4.5 percent

(Solmat3.to1)

**Table 8-6. Equivalent Costs of Thermal Energy from Solar
and Fossil Sources Combined Cycle Plants Using Natural Gas
($2.50 per Million Btu Natural Gas Price in 1995)**

Natural Gas Price Real Escalation Rate, %	Allowable Unit Heliostat Price, $m^2
-2	38
-1	47
0	57
1	68
2	81
3	98

**Table 8-7. Equivalent Costs of Thermal Energy from Solar
and Fossil Sources Pulverized Coal Plants Using Medium-Btu Coal
($1.25 per Million Btu Delivered Coal Price in 1995)**

Natural Gas Price Real Escalation Rate, %	Allowable Unit Heliostat Price, $m^2
-2	32
-1	36
0	42
1	48
2	55

8.2.2.3 Levelized Cost of Thermal Energy as a Function of Heliostat Price
The leveled cost of thermal energy from central receiver solar energy supply systems as a function of unit heliostat price is shown in **Table 8-8.** For these calculations, the central receiver facility consists of only the collector, receiver, and thermal storage systems.

**Table 8-8. Levelized Costs of Thermal Energy from a Central Receiver
Facility as a Function of Unit Heliostat Prices**

Unit Heliostat Price, $/m^2	Levelized Cost of Thermal Energy, $ Per Million Btu
60	3.40
80	3.90
100	4.40
120	4.90
140	5.40
160	5.90
180	6.40
200	6.90
220	7.30

(Solmat3.to1)

For points of reference, the estimated levelized costs of thermal energy for several options are as follows: $3.80 per million Btu for natural gas burned in a combined cycle power plant; $2.95 for coal burned in a pulverized coal power plant; and $7.10 for thermal energy from a parabolic trough solar collector field.

8.2.2.4 Market Position

A review of these data suggests several conclusions. First, solar-only central receiver plants will be a competitive option for bulk power generation in the southwestern United States when the cost of energy from new combined cycle power plants reaches $0.075/kWh$_e$. This should occur when natural gas prices reach $7 per million Btu, or environmental penalties for combustion emissions reach $0.035/kWh$_e$.

Second, the competitive solar-only central receiver plants will have a capacity of 200 MW$_e$, an annual capacity factor of 60 percent, an installed heliostat price Of $90/m^2 and a capital investment of $700 million. Reaching this heliostat price and raising this capital investment will not be possible without several precursor plants to establish a manufacturing base for the heliostats and to reduce the technical and financial risks in large nitrate salt systems.

Third, hybrid combined cycle-central receiver plants can be suitable precursor plants, for the following reasons:

- The levelized cost of energy can be within $0.01/kWh$_e$ to $0.02/kWh$_e$ of the cost of energy from a new combined cycle plant. The cost premium is a function of the annual solar energy contribution to the combined cycle plant.

- The collector system requires a reflector area of 200,000 m^2 to 400,000 m^2. This area is large enough to secure the cost benefits of components purchased in the thousands, but not so large as to require an enormous investment in mass production tooling.

- The high cost of solar thermal energy is partially offset by the low cost of fossil fuel energy- therefore, allowable heliostat prices can be as much as 30 percent greater than those required for a commercial solar-only plant. This can permit the establishment of a heliostat manufacturing business with a modest annual production level of perhaps 3,000 heliostats.

- The size of the receiver, thermal storage, and steam generation systems are within a factor of three to five times the size of the equipment at the Solar Two demonstration project. This provides a useful increase in the scale of the equipment, but does not incur excessive technical risks.

The energy subsidy of $0.01/kWh$_e$ to $0.02/lkWh$_e$, is required for two reasons. First, the levelized cost of solar thermal energy is greater than the cost of fossil energy, which increases the annual fuel costs for the plant. Second, gas turbine-generators suitable for integration with a central receiver facility require external silo combustors. Unfortunately, this combustor geometry does not produce the desired combination of high combustion temperatures and low oxides of nitrogen, which can be produced by the current generation of gas turbines with can-annular combustors. As a result, gas turbines with silo combustors are not as thermodynamically efficient as the latest generation of combined cycle equipment and are penalized with higher fuel use.

Fourth, a review of the allowable heliostat prices suggests that early target prices should be no greater than $120/kWh$_e$. Furthermore, designs or manufacturing approaches that can take costs below $100/m^2$ without the need for mass production quantities are necessary. Without reaching these targets, early market entry and broader market success will be very difficult to achieve.

The development of the first commercial central receiver projects will be assisted by the following:

- In markets where coal will dominate (China will build over 100,000 MW$_e$ of coal-fired power plants over the next decade), the benefits in the reduction of greenhouse gas emissions will be recognized and a premium will likely be paid for solar thermal energy.

- Many regions of the world do not have access to low-cost natural gas; where liquid fuels are used to power combined cycle plants, energy costs will be $0.06 to $0.07/kWh$_e$.

- The fuel diversity value of solar thermal energy will have market benefits. Countries such as Egypt, Mexico, and Khazakistan that have abundant gas supplies will look for ways to export natural gas to generate hard currency. Each of these countries has an excellent solar resource that could serve to increase exports of natural gas.

- Wind power plants offer low-cost bulk electric energy with no atmospheric emissions. However, wind power offers little or no capacity value, and capacity will be worth more than energy in the power markets of many developing countries.

These benefits will be tempered by the extremely competitive nature of bulk power markets in all regions where markets are sizable and of interest. Any premiums to be paid are likely to be modest, and other clean renewable options will compete in these markets.

8.2.3. Development of a Commercial Business
A commercial heliostat business will be developed through five steps, as follows:

- Market analysis. An analysis of the near-term and commercial markets for central receiver projects will define the annual demand, price requirements, and warranty requirements for heliostats. An initial evaluation is in the preceding sections.

- First commercial heliostat design and demonstration. A prototype heliostat which meets the needs of the near-term central receiver projects has been designed, fabricated, and tested in the course of the project. The design has demonstrated optical performance, verified the fabrication and installation procedures, and continued testing in the various locations is providing an indication of the reflector lifetime.

(Solmat3.to1)

- Marketing to near-term projects. Initial sales of heliostats will likely be made to a solar energy supply system consortium, which guarantees the annual supply of thermal energy by the central receiver facility to the electric power generation system. Sales to the consortium will be secured through a combination of aggressive pricing and performance warranties on the individual heliostats. In addition, the heliostat supplier will need to become a member of the consortium

- Commercial heliostat design and demonstration. Allowable heliostat costs for the commercial projects will be at least 25 percent less than the allowable costs for the near-term projects. This, in turn, will require an evolution in the heliostat design. A prototype heliostat will need to be designed, fabricated, and tested. This will demonstrate the optical performance, verify the fabrication procedures, and verify the reflector lifetime.

- Marketing to commercial projects. Sales in a commercial market will secured through a combination of technical advancements over competitive designs, aggressive pricing, and membership in the solar energy supply system consortium. The approach to this is presented in the following section.

8.3   Business Strategy

Development of a business strategy addresses the marketing of heliostats to both near-term and commercial central receiver projects.

8.3. 1. Marketing of Near-Term Projects
Marketing of the initial central receiver projects must resolve the issues of project financing and the supply of heliostats on a commercial basis.

8.3.1.1 Requirements for the Financing of Central Receiver Projects
Development of the initial commercial central receiver projects will require that the five issues associated with technical risk, guaranteed cost and schedule, non-recourse financing, guarantees and warranties, and requirements of the subsidizing organization be addressed.

The first requirement is minimum technical risk. Debt holders will likely require that the project exhibit a minimum of, and preferably zero technical risk. To this end, the plant should replicate the design and equipment sizes of the Solar Two project as closely as possible. However, commercial plants are not feasible at the $10\,MW_e$ size of the Solar Two project, and various technical risks will be involved in scaling the receiver, thermal storage tanks, and nitrate salt heat exchange equipment from the sizes required for the Solar Two project to the sizes required for the first commercial project. Component development programs will resolve a portion of the technical risk; however, it is anticipated that most of the risk will be borne by the equipment vendors in the form of performance guarantees.

The second requirement is a guaranteed capital cost and schedule. The project owners will likely require the engineer/constructor to provide a fixed-price bid for engineering, procurement, construction, startup, and to guarantee a date for the start of commercial operations. It should be noted that capital cost premiums could be expected on new equipment items. For example,

(Solmat3.to1)

recovery of the initial engineering costs and performance guarantees for the nitrate salt heat exchange equipment will result in equipment costs that are higher for the first than the fifth plant. Component development programs will help to reduce the cost premiums; however, it is anticipated that most of the premiums will be passed through the facility investors in the form of higher capital costs.

The third requirement is non-recourse financing, in which the debt holders have recourse only to the cash flow and capital assets of the project if the project fails to perform. This is currently the standard approach to power plant financing. If the debt holders will be unwilling to assume any portion of the technical risk, including the performance of first-of-a-kind equipment, then the risk of poor solar facility performance will be borne by the equity investors in the form of reduced returns.

The fourth requirement is performance guarantees and warranties. Demonstration by the engineer/constructor of the design point performance immediately following construction will be required. However, once the tests have been completed, the engineer/constructor assumes no further responsibility for the plant performance. Consequently, the debt holders will likely insist on equipment guarantees and an annual performance warranty. Guarantees to service the debt in the event of a one-time equipment failure or extraordinary circumstances, such as a 100-year storm, can be made by establishing a capital reserve account or an insurance policy. However, the size of the account or policy coverage is typically limited to debt service for a period of 6 months to 1 year, and it is prohibitively expensive to insure the annual performance for the life of the debt. An annual performance warranty, which guarantees payments to the debt holders over the some portion of the life of the debt, is often feasible. This may be secured by a line of credit from a bank or perhaps a power purchase agreement with a local utility, which adjusts the energy payments in response to the plant performance.

The fifth requirement is the satisfaction of any requirements, which a subsidizing organization might place on the project. It is generally believed that the first, or perhaps first few, commercial projects will require a subsidy in the form of a capital grant or energy production credit. The subsidizing agency will, in all likelihood, place some requirements on the size, capacity factor, and annual solar energy contribution. or capital cost.

8.3.1.2 Requirements for the Supply of Heliostats
Under the concept described below in Section 8.3.3, Role of the Solar Energy Supply System Consortium, an organization is formed which guarantees the annual supply of thermal energy from the central receiver facility to the electric power generation system. It is anticipated that the heliostat supplier will become a member of, and sell heliostats to, the consortium.

Sales of heliostats will be secured through a combination of aggressive pricing and performance Warranties on the individual heliostats. Aggressive pricing will be required for two reasons: first, a reduction in the cost of the collector system will significantly reduce the capital cost of the plant; and second, competition among potential heliostat suppliers is expected to be keen.

Warranties on the following items will also be required to meet the requirements of the consortium and the project investors:

- Optical quality, including clean mirror reflectivity (for example, 93 percent ±1 percent), reflected beam size (all of the flux with an intensity greater than or equal to 10 percent of the peak flux contained within a circle with a diameter of 14 milliradians), beam shape (1.4 milliradian total error, including both the mirror module slope effort and the pointing error), and tracking accuracy (3.3 milliradians with a wind speed of 12 meters per second).

- Component reliability of at least 99 percent during the one-year warranty period.

- Heliostat controller and heliostat array controller software that operates, and communicates with system, as intended.

8.3.2. Marketing of Commercial Projects

Marketing of the commercial central receiver projects must resolve the issues of project financing and the supply of heliostats on a commercial basis.

8.3.2.1 Requirements for the Financing of Central Receiver Projects

Development of commercial central receiver projects will require that the four issues associated with technical risk, guaranteed cost and schedule, non-recourse financing, and guarantees and warranties are addressed.

The first requirement is minimum technical risk. Debt holders will likely require that the project exhibit zero technical risk. To this end, the plant should replicate the design and equipment sizes of the initial commercial projects as closely as possible. However, solar-only plants may not be feasible at sizes below 200 MW_e, and various technical risks will be involved in scaling the receiver, thermal storage tanks, and nitrate salt heat exchange equipment from the sizes required for the initial commercial projects to the sizes required for the 200 MW_e project. Component development programs will resolve a portion of the technical risk; however, it is anticipated that most of the risk will be borne by the equipment vendors in the form of performance guarantees.

The second, third, and fourth requirements are, respectively, guaranteed capital cost and schedule, non-recourse funding, and performance guarantees and warranties. The requirements for commercial solar-only projects are likely to be similar to the initial commercial projects discussed above.

8.3.2.2 Requirements for the Supply of Commercial Heliostats

As with the initial commercial projects, it is anticipated that sales of heliostats will be made to the solar energy supply system consortium. Heliostats for use in commercial projects will be available from a number of competitive suppliers, and can be viewed essentially as commodities. As such, various technical features will be needed to differentiate one supplier from another. These features might include performance warranties extending beyond one year, a reflector material with a 50-year lifetime, drives which do not require routine maintenance, automatic defocusing to convex reflector shapes following a loss of site power, unusually low electric energy consumption for the membrane focus control system and heliostat controller, cleaning methods which do not require water, or heliostat controller memories which are immune to interruptions in the electric power.

105

8.3.3. Role of the Solar Energy Supply System Consortium

A promising approach to the financing and ownership of a central receiver project is the division of the plant into two separate facilities. The first facility is the solar energy supply system, which includes the collector system, receiver system, thermal storage tanks and inventory, nitrate salt heat exchangers, and associated controls. The second facility is the electric power generation system, which includes the gas turbine-generator (if applicable), steam turbine-generator, balance of plant, and associated controls. Each facility is independent of the other, to the extent that each is financially separately and has separate operation and maintenance staffs.

A consortium of organizations is formed to finance, design, install, and warrant the performance of the solar energy supply system. The consortium may consist of one, some, or all of the following organizations: architect/engineer, heliostat supplier, receiver supplier, thermal storage tank vendor, nitrate salt heat exchanger vendor, nitrate salt supplier, project investors, project owner, and a third party. A separate consortium of organizations is formed to finance, design, install, and warrant the performance of the electric power generation system. The consortium may consist of one, some, or all of the following organizations: architect/engineer, gas- or steam-turbine supplier, project investors, project owner, and a third party.

The electric power generation system sends feedwater, and in some cases compressed air, to the solar energy supply system. Thermal energy is transferred to the feedwater and the compressed air in the solar energy supply system, and saturated steam and hot compressed air are returned to the electric power generation system. The electric power generation system has a take-or-pay contract for the thermal energy from the solar energy supply system.

There are five compelling motivations to this arrangement. First, the following items are the responsibility of one organization: design, capital cost, construction schedule, annual performance, and annual operation and maintenance cost. This greatly simplifies the task of assigning responsibility for warranty and guarantee issues, and reduces the financial uncertainties to project investors.

Second, the electric power generation system can treat the cost of thermal energy from the central receiver facility as a fuel expense. This allows the capital investment in the central receiver plant to be treated as an operating expense by the combined cycle plant, which reduces the taxable income and tax liability of the combined cycle plant. Some portion of this benefit is returned to the solar energy supply system in the form of larger payments for the thermal energy. This is a significant economic benefit to the overall project, and compensates for some of the tax disadvantages, which a renewable energy facility normally faces if the entire investment in fuel is treated as a capital investment.

Third, the separate facilities are financed from separate funding sources. This allows the optimum combination of debt fraction, debt interest rate, equity fraction, return on equity and escalation rate in the energy sales price to be selected for each facility.

106

Fourth, the thermal and financial performance of the central receiver facility, which involves the largest uncertainties, is easily separated from the thermal and financial performance of the electric power generation system. This makes the financial performance of the overall plant transparent to all of the investors.

Fifth, if the solar energy supply system operates reliably, the annual revenues to the system are guaranteed by the take-or-pay contract with the electric power generation system. The only risk in this arrangement is the annual availability of the electric power plant. However, current plants demonstrate availability's of 95 percent and greater, and the anticipated performance risk is minimal.

It is anticipated that the annual performance of the central receiver facility will need to be guaranteed by the solar energy supply system consortium in a manner similar to that used by Luz International Limited in the Solar Electric Generating System parabolic trough solar power plants. In the Luz projects, the annual solar thermal energy delivered to the turbine-generator was guaranteed to be a function of the annual direct normal radiation. To this end, the following issues regarding a performance warranty for a central receiver solar energy supply system become important:

- There is the strong likelihood that a variation in the annual direct normal radiation of plus or minus 10 percent from the long-term average will occur due to the absence or presence, respectively, of recent volcanic activity. An escrow account for the payments from the electric power generation system to the solar energy supply system may need to be established to remove the annual variations in cash flows.

- The annual thermal energy delivered by the receiver is a strong function of the accuracy of the heliostat mirror modules canting (if applicable), accuracy of the heliostat pointing vectors, reflectivity of the mirrors, and absorbtivity of the receiver tube coating. Ideally, the incident flux on the receiver can be continuously measured, such that any deficiency in the energy delivered can be traced to either the collector or the receiver system. However, instrumentation which can map the incident flux on the receiver, with an accuracy sufficient to resolve warranty questions, does not exist. The consortium must guarantee the combined performance of the collector and receiver systems, but will need to make an internal decision regarding the distribution of liabilities among the component vendors.

- Over the past fifteen years, a data base on component efficiency and reliability has been compiled from the operation of the Solar One project, component and system tests at Sandia National Laboratories, and research programs at the National Renewable Energy Laboratory. In addition, new data will become available over the next three years from the Solar Two project. However, much of the data are based on operating times measured in hundreds of hours, whereas performance warranties for commercial projects need to address operating times in tens of thousands of hours. As a result, the consortium will need to estimate equipment and system reliabilities based on significant extrapolations of the data.

(Solmat3.to1)

8.4 Market Analysis

Possible medium and long term markets for heliostats, listing a potential customer, power plant project, required heliostat selling price, marketing approach, and required heliostat development, are outlined below.

8.4.1 Market Opportunity Number1
Customer: International Technology Development Projects

Project: In 1993, Israel expressed an interest in central receiver facilities which could supply superheated steam to various process industries in the Negev Desert, and thereby reduce the use of heavy fuel oil as a heat source. One example uses a 30 MW_t water/steam central receiver to supply a magnesium reduction plant at the Dead Sea Works. The collector system would require 590 100 m^2 stretched membrane heliostats for a total collector area of 59,000 m^2.

Allowable Heliostat Price: The levelized cost of fuel oil in Israel is likely to be in the range of $8 to S10 per million Btu. In 1993, the government of Israel offered a construction grant equal to 38 percent of the plant capital cost for projects in Development Zone A. If a central receiver project can offer a levelized cost of thermal energy in the range of $13 to $16 per million Btu (equivalent to $8 to $10 per million Btu with the subsidy), solar energy systems should be competitive with fuel oil. Although this cost target appears generous, the small size of the solar energy system together with relatively high operation and maintenance costs yields allowable collector system cost in the range of only $60 to $120/$m^2$.

Marketing Approach: To supply heliostats to this project, a manufacturer must displace Boeing Corporation as the likely heliostat vendor by offering an aggressive heliostat price and an annual performance guarantee for the collector system.

Required Heliostat Development: A small market such as a Dead Sea Works project cannot justify a development effort to meet a required heliostat price. In effect, the levelized cost of fuel oil defines the allowable heliostat price; only if the heliostat designs available meet the price requirements can the central receiver project proceed.

Heliostat Installation Date: Heliostat installation can proceed 18 months after the start of the final design activities.

8.4.2 Market Opportunity Number 2
Customer: Central Receiver Development Consortium

Project: A 175 MW_e combined cycle-central receiver project at the Solar Enterprise Zone appears to be technically and economically feasible. The collector system would require 1,965 140 m^2 stretched membrane heliostats, for a total collector area of 275,000 m^2. The project depends, in part-, on securing power sales and transmission contracts that enable sales of the energy for $0.05/$kWh_e$ to $0.06/$kWh_e$. The Corporation for Solar Technology and Renewable

Resources (CSTRR) is a private organization which has been established to assist in securing power sales agreements for projects at the Solar Enterprise Zone.

Allowable Heliostat Price: In an informal proposal to CSTRR, the proposed central receiver facility supplied 12 percent of the annual demand of the combined cycle plant. With an energy contribution of this size, the levelized cost of energy from the combined cycle plant is not particularly sensitive to the unit cost of the heliostats. However, the solicitation for the Solar Enterprise Zone is competitive, and every avenue for reducing the cost of energy must be pursued. Although the economic analysis in the proposal was based on a unit heliostat cost of $120/ m^2, the levelized cost of thermal energy from the central receiver facility was $14 per million Btu. Therefore, the allowable price cannot exceed, and should preferably be less than, $120/ m^2.

Marketing Approach: The prospects for this project depend to a large degree on the ability of CSTRR to secure a federal customer for the electric energy. If a long-term contract with a customer offering to pay $0.06/kWh$_e$ can be signed, a project can likely be undertaken following conventional approaches to project development.

The plant is divided into two facilities, as follows, to apportion risk among the investors:

- A solar energy supply system, consisting of the collector system, receiver system, thermal storage system, nitrate salt-to-compressed air heat exchanger, and nitrate salt-to-water/steam evaporator. A company or group of companies provides an annual performance guarantee.

- A conventional combined cycle power plant, which purchases natural gas from the local gas utility, hot compressed air from the central receiver facility, and superheated steam from the central receiver facility.

Required Heliostat Development: The heliostat development activities under Phases I and II of the SolMaT Initiative have resulted in a design with an installed cost of $157/m 2 ; therefore, development activities will continue in support of the Solar Enterprise Zone project.

8.4.3 Market Opportunity Number 3
Customer: Global Environmental Facility of the World Bank

Project: A grant of $50 million from the Global Environmental Facility is probably sufficient to design and install the collector, receiver, thermal storage, and steam generation systems in a 40 MW$_t$ central receiver facility. The facility would be located adjacent to an existing coal-fired power plant, and would supply superheated steam to the conventional plant to reduce the use of coal and the emissions of carbon dioxide. The collector system would require 800 100 m^2 stretched membrane heliostats, for a total collector area of 80,000 m^2. With direct normal radiation comparable to that in Barstow, California, (2,707 kWh/m^2), 370,000 million Btu of solar energy are available each year, which would displace 23,000 tons of coal. If the savings in coal fuel costs are equal to the incremental central receiver facility operation and maintenance

(Solmat3.to1)

costs, the plant owners should be neutral to the addition of the central receiver facility. International Solar Plan markets include India, China, Pakistan, Israel, Egypt, Jordan, South Africa, Brazil, and Chile.

Allowable Heliostat Price: The purpose of the grant from the Global Environmental Facility is to reduce the emissions of carbon dioxide. To reduce the emissions to the maximum extent possible, and thereby increase the interest of the Global Environmental Facility, it is vital to minimize the unit cost ($/kW$_t$) of the central receiver facility because 1) the size of the grant is fixed and 2) the reduction in emissions is directly proportional to the thermal rating of the plant. Unit heliostat prices must be no greater, and preferably less, than the $120/m^2 postulated for the Solar Enterprise Zone to secure the interest of the World Bank.

Marketing Approach: International activities under the Solar Plan should identify one or more coal-fired power plants suitable for repowering by a central receiver facility. Once a candidate project is selected, standard project development activities can be pursued. It is anticipated that an annual performance guarantee for the collector and receiver systems will need to be offered.

Required Heliostat Development: A design with an installed cost no greater than $120/m^2; will be required in support of the Global Environmental Facility project.

8.4.4 Market Opportunity Number 4
Customer: Global Environmental Facility of the World Bank

Project: A grant of $50 million from the Global Environmental Facility is sufficient to subsidize one half of the $100 million capital cost of the collector, receiver, thermal storage, nitrate salt heat exchange systems in a 145 MW$_t$ central receiver facility. The facility would be located adjacent to a 180 Mew combined cycle plant, and would supply high-temperature compressed air and superheated steam to the gas and steam turbines, respectively. The collector system would require 2,900 150 m^2 stretched-membrane heliostats, for a total collector area of 275,000 m^2. With direct normal radiation comparable to that in Barstow, California, the annual solar energy delivered to the combined cycle plant is 1,000,000 million Btu, which reduces the fossil fuel use by 12 percent. A capital cost subsidy of 50 percent reduces the cost of solar energy to approximately the levelized cost of liquid fossil fuel in a developing country. Under these conditions, the plant owners should be neutral to the addition of the central receiver facility.

Allowable Heliostat Price: The purpose of the grant from the Global Environmental Facility is to reduce fossil energy use, and thereby the emissions of carbon dioxide. To reduce the emissions to the maximum extent possible, and thereby increase the interest of the Global Environmental Facility, it is vital to minimize the unit cost ($/kW$_t$) of the central receiver facility because 1) the size of the grant is fixed and 2) the reduction in sessions is directly proportional to the thermal rating of the plant. Unit heliostat prices must be no greater, and preferably less, than the $120/m^2 postulated for the Solar Enterprise Zone to secure the interest of the World Bank.

Marketing Approach: International activities under the SolarPlan should identify one or more sites suitable for the combined cycle-central receiver concept. Once a candidate project is

(Solmat3.to1)

selected, standard project development activities can be pursued. It is anticipated that an annual performance guarantee for the collector and receiver systems will need to be offered.

Required Heliostat Development: A design with an installed cost no greater than $120/m^2$; will be required in support of the Global Environmental Facility project.

8.4.5 Market Opportunity Number 5
Customer: International Central Receiver Consortium

Project: The European PHOEBUS Consortium has tentative plans to build a 30 MW hybrid solar/fossil fuel project in the Middle East or North Africa using an 80 MW_t volumetric air receiver and a Rankine cycle power plant. The collector system would require 1180 140 m^2 stretched membrane heliostats, for a total collector area of 165,000 in

Marketing Approach: To supply heliostats to this project, a U.S. manufacturer must first join the Consortium and then displace the Spanish research organization Centro de Investigaciones Energ6ticas, Medioamblentalcs y Tecnol6gicas (CIEMAT) as the preferred heliostat vendor. This might be achieved through a combination of aggressive pricing and the offer of an annual performance guarantee for the collector system.

Allowable Heliostat Price: The Post-Feasibility Study IC report prepared by the Technology Program for the Solar Air Receiver (TSA) Consortium shows an installed collector system cost of $200/m^2$. If an U. S. manufacturer could offer a system with an installed cost of $120/m^2$, this would reduce the capital cost of the plant by one-eighth and may be sufficient to displace the Spanish heliostat vendor.

Required Heliostat Development: If one or more U.S. central receiver projects precede the PHOEBUS project, domestic heliostat technology will be further advanced than the Spanish designs. Development activities may be limited to accommodating site specific requirements for local manufacturing content, soils bearing stresses, or wind speeds.

8.4.6 Market Opportunity Number 6
Customer: Independent Power Producers

Project: The early domestic and international central receiver projects will likely be combined cycle-central receiver plants. Moderate capital or operating cost subsidies will compensate for the displacement of perhaps one-eighth of the fossil energy by relatively expensive solar energy. However, these subsidies will not be available indefinitely and the technology must eventually make the transition to solar-only plants.

When installed heliostat prices fall below $80/m^2$ to $90/m^2$, and the cost of energy from new fossil-fired power plants rises above $0.06/kWh_e$ 200 MW_e solar-only plants will be a competitive option for independent power producers. If one 200 MW_e plant is built each year, the annual demand for heliostats will be 13,000 and 1,800,000 m, respectively.

(Solmat3.to1)

Allowable Heliostat Price: Installed prices will need to be in the range of $80/m^2 to $90/m^2 for solar-only central receiver projects to be commercially feasible.

Marketing Approach: When solar-only plants are a commercial option, the technology will have developed to the point where the performance and financial risks are well defined. Consequently, an independent power producer can develop a project using conventional financing approaches.

Required Heliostat Development: It is anticipated that unit heliostat prices will be approximately $100/m^2 following the completion of medium-term projects described above; therefore, a reduction of 10 to 20 percent will be necessary to meet the required price in a commercial market. It is reasonable to expect that a heliostat market will have developed to the point where some portion of the cost reduction can be accomplished by mass production. The balance of the reduction will need to be achieved through a combination of the following:

Project Commitment Anticipated: Based on current estimates of natural gas price escalation rates, solar-only projects should be a competitive option in the 2005 to 2010 time frame.

8.4.7 Results of Market Analysis and Business Hypothesis
A summary of the market analysis is illustrated in **Figure 8-3**. Shown are the annual demand for heliostats, and the required unit-selling price, for the period from 1997 to the first commercial 200 MW/m^2 projects starting on or about 2007. A review of the market analysis, together with the information on required heliostat prices developed in Section II - Business Hypothesis, leads to the following conclusions:

- The average annual demand of heliostats in the early-subsidized projects is approximately 1,000, jumping quickly to over 10,000 when the first commercial projects become a competitive option.

- Heliostat prices must fall rapidly from the approximately $800/m^2 anticipated for the four heliostats in Phase II of the SolMaT initiative to the range of $120/m^2 to $140/m^2 for the early subsidized projects if thermal energy from a central receiver, which will carry a premium for financial risk, is to be selected in preference to thermal energy from a parabolic trough collector field. This decrease in price will be aided by only a limited cumulative heliostat production.

- Heliostat prices must be in the range of $80/m^2 to $90/m^2 if solar-only, plants are to be competitive in the commercial electric energy market.

112

(Solmat3.to1)

**Figure 8-3. Annual Heliostat Production Rate and Required
Selling Price as a Function of Time**

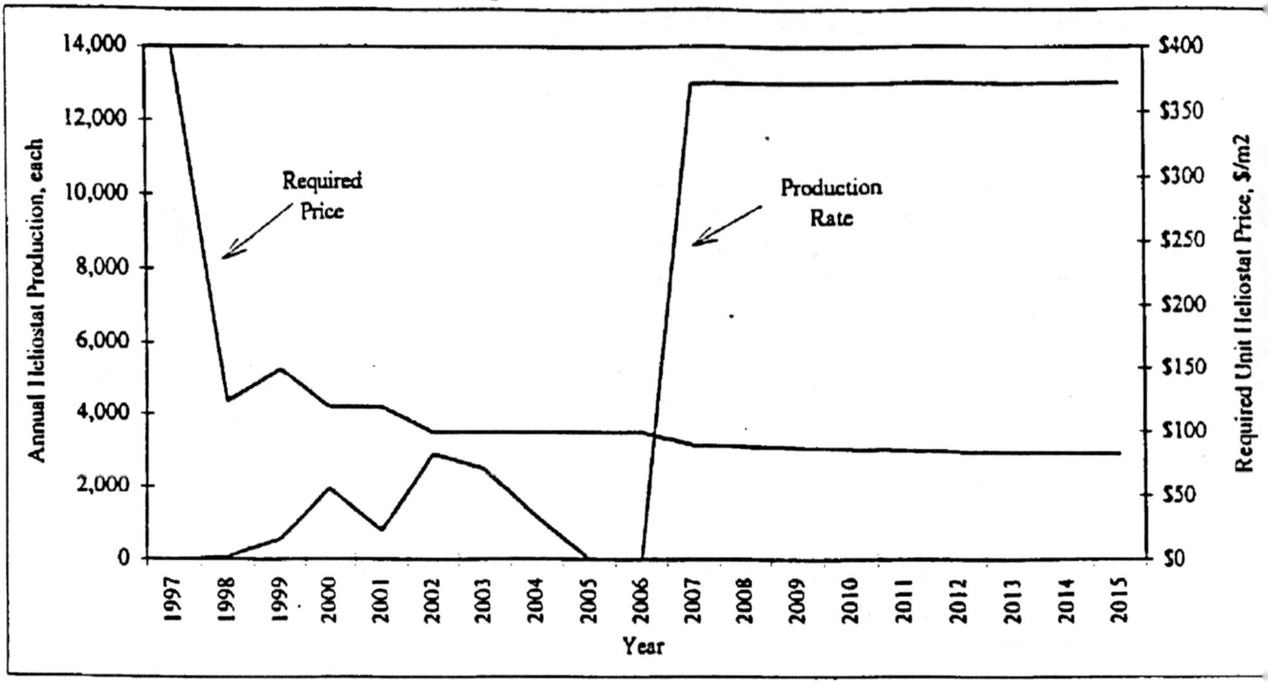

8.5   Manufacturing Strategy

8.5. 1. Design-to-Cost Approach
As outlined in Section 8.2, Business Hypothesis, the first commercial central receiver projects
could be combined cycle-central receiver plants, with a requirement of 2,000 to perhaps 4,000
heliostats in each plant. Allowable heliostat prices are in the range of $120/m^2$ to $135/m^2$. The
long-term commercial central receiver projects will be 200 MW, solar-only Rankine cycle power
plants, with a requirement 15,000 to 25,000 heliostats in each plant. Allowable heliostat prices
are likely to be in the range of $80/m^2$ to $90/m^2$

To meet these separate market needs, two approaches to heliostat manufacturing need to be
developed. The first approach should minimize installed heliostat prices for annual production
volumes of several thousand, and the second should minimize prices for volumes of several tens of
thousands. In each approach, the price includes the engineering, materials, fabrication labor,
shipping, installation labor, and amortization of tooling for each heliostat.

8.5.2. Early Production Approach
The early production heliostat consists of the following components:

• Combination foundation and pedestal pipe

113

(Solmat3.tol)

- Azimuth and elevation drive, located at the top of the pedestal

- Module support structure, consisting of two steel pipe torque tubes, bolted to the drive, and four steel wire trusses, welded to the torque tubes

- 22 stretched membrane mirror modules, bolted to the trusses. Each module has a reflector diameter of 3.2 m, which provides a total reflector area of 170 m². Glued to the front membrane of each mirror module are six mirror tiles that are trimmed to fit the perimeter of the circular membrane. The tiles are a second-surface silvered-glass mirror.

- Heliostat controller, located at the base of the pedestal

- Buried wiring, providing electric power, control signals, and grounding to each heliostat

- Central heliostat array controller, determining pointing vectors for each heliostat.

8.5.2.1 Mirror Module

The nominal module diameter of 3 meters was selected for four reasons. First, the modules are small enough to be fabricated in a factory, including the placement of the mirror tiles, and then shipped to the site. This increases the content of factory labor, which typically has a high productivity, and reduces the content of the field labor, which often has a low productivity. Second, the cost of tooling to fabricate a small module is less than the cost to fabricate a large module. This should reduce the unit tooling costs because there are a limited number of square meters over which to amortize the tooling. Third, all of the fabrication tooling remains in one central facility and does not need to be moved from plant site to plant site. This should also help to reduce the unit tooling costs. Fourth, stretched membrane modules typically operate with a slight vacuum in the plenum between membranes. The vacuum causes the membranes to assume a quasi-spherical shape, which focuses the reflected image on the receiver. However, the size of the reflected image from a module 3 meters in diameter is small enough such that the front membrane can remain flat. This eliminates the need for a focus control system on each module. It should be noted that a module with a diameter of 3 meters has a higher unit weight (lb./m² than a module with a diameter of 15 meters. In commercial quantities, the higher unit weight will translate into a higher unit cost. However, for the limited production quantities envisioned for the first commercial projects, the sum of the material, assembly, and tooling amortization costs for the small module should be less than for the large module.

8.5.2.2 Reflector

The selection of glass mirror tiles, rather than a silvered polymer film such as ECP-305, for the reflector surface follows a similar line of reasoning. In theory, the polymer film should offer a number of significant advantages. First, the film has a reflectivity of 95 percent, which is 4 percentage points higher than the glass mirrors; this should reduce the cost of the collector system by just over 4 percent. Second, the film can be glued by machine to the front membrane; this offers a significant cost savings compared to the manual labor operations of cutting and gluing the glass mirror tiles. Third, the projected cost of the polymer film is in the range of $5/m² to $20/m², which is one-eighth to one-half of the present cost of the glass mirrors.

(Solmat3.to1)

In practice, the polymer film suffers from a problem which, in its present form, makes it unacceptable for commercial use. The polymethylmethacrylate acrylic film absorbs water from rain, dew, and moisture from the air, and this water both swells the film and corrodes the silver. The latter effect limits the reflector lifetime to perhaps five years, at which time the film must be replaced. However, glues with a powerful adhesive are required to prevent the film from breaking the bond with the membrane. Removal of the old film without damaging the thin steel membrane, and installation of new film in the field, has yet to be demonstrated in a commercial operation. As a result, the use of a polymer reflector film must be considered premature, and glass mirror tiles have been selected for early commercial applications.

8.5.2.3 Drive
The structure to support an array of 22 stretched membrane modules for a 170 m^2 heliostat differs little from the structure to support the 25 glass/metal mirror modules on the 148.6 m^2 heliostat by Advanced Thermal Systems. With similar support structures, the conventional combination azimuth and elevation drive is a logical choice.

Two approaches to the drive design are possible. The first approach is the manufacture of a specialty drive developed specifically for a heliostat. At least 2,700 specialty drives, including the 1,818 used by Martin Marietta Corporation in the Solar One project and the 860 used by ARCO Solar Incorporated in the Hesperia and Carrisa Plains photovoltaic power plants, have been built. All of the drives have operated reliably for periods up to 6 years, and many approaching 10 years. This drive is a proven concept, and competitive designs are available from several commercial manufacturers.

The second approach is the use of commercial speed reduction drives in series to meet the needs of the heliostat. For example, the separate elevation and azimuth drives can each be performed by a combination of an input drive using a Dodge Adaptable Tigear worm-helical gear drive with a ratio of 25:1, an intermediate drive using a Dodge Combination Tigear double reduction worm-helical gear drive with a ratio of 30:1, and an output drive using a Dodge TXT torque arm reducer double reduction helical gear drive with a ratio of 25:1. The three gearboxes in series provide an overall reduction ratio of 18,750:1.

It is anticipated that both the specialty drive and the combination of commercial drives will exhibit comparable reliabilities. Therefore, the choice between the type of drives will be based on the lowest capital cost.

8.5.2.4 Foundation
The use of a combination azimuth and elevation drive leads to the selection of a steel pipe for the common pedestal and foundation. The pipe is placed in an augered hole, and concrete is poured around the pipe to complete the foundation.

8.5.2.5 Controls and Field Wiring
The control system includes the heliostat array controller, heliostat controller, and field control wiring. The heliostat array controller is a central computer, which responds to plant operating mode commands, periodically computes the sun position, and periodically calculates the new pointing vector for each heliostat. The heliostat controller is a small microprocessor, one of which is included with each heliostat, that interprets commands from the array controller, and

115

controls the motion of the azimuth and elevation drive motors to point the heliostat in the correct direction.

The division of computational duties between the heliostat array controller and the heliostat controller is somewhat arbitrary. However, fast personal computers can currently perform the pointing vector calculations for the heliostat field in a commercial plant. Therefore, the lowest costs are likely to be achieved with a central array controller which performs as many calculations as possible, and a heliostat controller that performs little more than a count of motor revolutions.

Two approaches to the supply of electric power and control signals to each heliostat have been considered. The first is the conventional approach of buried electric power and control wiring, which has been used successfully on the heliostat fields at Solar One, Hesperia, and Carrisa Plains. The second is the autonomous heliostat, which uses a photovoltaic panel and battery for electric power and a radio receiver and transmitter for communication. For the first commercial plants, the conventional approach is preferred in terms of reliability, capital cost, and operating cost.

8.5.3 Commercial Production Approach
The commercial production heliostat consists of the following components:

- Circular concrete grade beam foundation, with a diameter equal to the diameter of the reflector

- Steel pedestal legs, with wheels at the bottom, supporting the reflector at the centerline

- Azimuth drive is a motor driving one of the wheels along the circular foundation, and the elevation drive is a centerless drive with a large drive wheel and a small motor/gear drive.

- One stretched membrane mirror module, with a diameter of 13.8 m and an area of 150 m^2. The reflector is a first-surface silver mirror, with an aluminum oxide or carbon surface coating to provide protection from wash abrasion and water corrosion

- Heliostat controller, located at the base of the pedestal

- Buried wiring, providing electric power, control signals, and grounding to each heliostat

- Central heliostat array controller, determining pointing vectors for each heliostat.

8.5.3.1 *Mirror Module*
A heliostat, composed of one reflector with an area of 150 m^2, was selected for two reasons. First, the unit weight (lb/m^2) of the module decreases with increasing diameter. Given mature fabrication methods, the reduction in unit weight translates into a reduction in unit cost. Therefore, the heliostat should use the minimum number of reflector modules; in this case, one. Second, this characteristic should be exploited until the size of the reflected image reaches the

(Solmat3.to1)

point where the marginal cost reduction due to an increase in reflector area is equal to the marginal cost increase due to an increase in spillage losses at the receiver surface. This reflector size is currently judged to be 150 m^2.

A reflector area of 150 m^2 results is a module diameter of 13.8 m, which is too large for factory assembly and shipping-therefore, the fabrication facility must be located at the project site. This has three disadvantages compared to the fabrication of the three-meter-diameter modules in the early production approach. First, field fabrication increases the content of field labor, which often has a low productivity, and reduces the content of the factory labor, which typically has a high productivity. Second, the cost of tooling to fabricate a large module will be much higher than the cost to fabricate a small module. Third, all of the fabrication tooling must be moved from plant site to plant site, and mobile tooling equipment will be more expensive than stationary equipment. However, for the annual production quantities envisioned for commercial projects, it is believed that the significant savings in material costs for the large module will more than offset the increased field labor and tooling costs.

It should be noted that a reflector with a diameter of 13.8 in requires focusing to prevent excessive spillage losses at the receiver; therefore, a focus control system must be part of each heliostat.

8.5.3.2 Reflector

An experimental reflector, consisting of a first-surface silver mirror applied directly to the stainless steel membrane and protected with a transparent hard coating, is postulated for the commercial heliostat.

Two potential reflector designs are under development at the National Renewable Energy Laboratory. The first consists of the following: a substrate of polyethylene teraphthallate (Mylae), which is approximately 500,000 nanometers thick; a second layer of copper, which is 70 nanometers thick; a third layer of silver, which is 140 nanometers thick; and a protective fourth layer of aluminum oxide, which is 5,200 nanometers thick.

The second reflector design consists of the following: a substrate of polyethylene teraphthallate, which is approximately 500,000 nanometers thick; a second layer of a proprietary bonding material; a third layer of silver, which is 140 nanometers thick; a fourth layer of a proprietary bonding material; a fifth inner layer of "diamond-like" carbon, which is 500 to 2,000 nanometers thick; and a sixth outer layer of diamond-like carbon, which is 1 to 10 nanometers thick. The inner layer has an optical transmittance and hardness comparable to low-iron glass. The outer layer has an optical transmittance and hardness equivalent to float glass and comparable to diamonds, respectively.

Note that both reflectors are applied to a Mylar substrate rather than stainless steel; the plastic provides the smooth surface required for a high specular reflectivity. The surface imperfections in a rolled steel sheet need to be covered and smoothed; this is the subject of a separate research effort.

These reflective surfaces offer four important features. First, the ceramic or carbon coating provides a non-hygroscopic surface, which protects the silver from corrosion due to moisture and

117

provides a reflector life of 30 years. Second, the surfaces are highly resistant to abrasion and permit reizular mechanical cleaning without scratching. Third, the unit material requirements (lb_m/m^2) are extremely low, which contributes to a low reflector cost. Fourth, application of the reflector surfaces is performed by machine, which eliminates the field labor costs for cutting and gluing glass mirror tiles to the membranes. Costs for each reflector surface, in commercial quantities of 100,000 m^2 per year, are projected to be less than $10/m^2$. This compares very favorably with the current material cost of glass mirror tiles and adhesive of $50/m^2$ in admittedly small quantities.

This reflector surface has been demonstrated on laboratory samples with areas of approximately 0.5 square feet, and small samples have shown promising projected lifetimes in accelerated weathering tests at the National Renewable Energy Laboratory. Uniform application of the coatings over large surface areas has yet to be demonstrated. Nonetheless, a reflector with these or similar characteristics is needed if the commercial heliostat is to reach the cost goals of $80/m^2$ to $90/m^2$.

8.5.3.3 Drive

One of the theoretical advantages of a stretched membrane reflector is the use of large, thin membranes supported in tension by a perimeter ring in compression. Transferring the gravity and wind loads from the perimeter to a central drive in the form of bending loads in two or three torque tubes is not an efficient use of structural materials. In theory, the support structure and drive should operate on the perimeter ring. The drive must also allow the reflector to stow facing down. This reduces dirt accumulation at night and minimizes denting of the reflector due to hail.

One approach to a perimeter support uses steel pedestal legs, with wheels at the bottom, supporting the reflector at the perimeter centerline. The perimeter drive arrangement could use an azimuth motor driving one or more of the wheels along a circular foundation track. The elevation drive uses a large-diameter drive wheel attached to the heliostat ring.

Care must be taken in the design of the perimeter support structure and drives to ensure that the theoretical cost benefits are realized. For example, slippage in a drive cable may preclude the use of Hall-effect sensors on the drive motor to determine heliostat position. As a result, a more expensive arrangement using a light emitting diode and receiver, which looks through teeth mounted periodically on the perimeter ring, may be required.

8.5.3.4 Foundation

If the heliostat is supported at the perimeter, the foundation will likely be circular concrete grade beam with a diameter equal to the diameter of the reflector. Again, care must be taken to ensure that the theoretical cost benefits are realized. For example, the labor and material costs for the trench, concrete, and reinforcing steel in the grade beam are likely to be more expensive than the auger and grout costs for a steel pipe foundation. This is particularly true if the reinforcing steel must be bent in the field to the radius of curvature of the grade beam.

8.5.3.5 Controls and Field Wiring

The design of the control system for the heliostat field in a commercial plant will likely be the same as that used in the early production plants. Specifically, the lowest costs are likely to be

118

achieved with a central array controller which performs as many calculations as possible, and a heliostat controller that performs little more than a count of motor revolutions.

The concept of an autonomous heliostat, which uses a photovoltaic panel and battery for electric power and a radio receiver and transmitter for communication, may have merit for commercial installations. However, two prerequisites must be satisfied. First, photovoltaic panel prices must be in the range of $1 to $2 per Watt. Second, batteries must be available that have a life of at least 15 years in the temperatures encountered at a desert location, and that are of a reasonable cost. If these conditions cannot be met, the conventional approach of buried power and control wiring will be preferred in terms of reliability, capital cost, and operating cost.

8.5.4 Supplier Alliances

The number and degree of alliances between the heliostat manufacturer and component suppliers will depend on the heliostat design and annual production volume. In general, alliances should be pursued for those components, which can be provided at a lower cost or where warranty obligations will be passed through to the supplier.

8.5.4.1 Early Production Heliostat
Supplier alliances for the early production heliostats will likely be limited to the drives. Several manufacturers can supply a combination azimuth and elevation drive on a competitive basis. However, an alliance with one of the manufacturers could reduce the price through a cost-sharing agreement that granted an exclusive supply contract on subsequent projects.

Two vendors have an exclusive position for the supply of components to the early production heliostats. Allegheny-Ludlum is currently the only vendor, which rolls stainless steel strips in both the longitudinal and transverse directions to meet the requirements for consistent thickness. Similarly, Naugatuck Glass is the only supplier of glass mirror tiles, which are 1.0 mm thick.

The heliostat controllers can be manufactured by Science Applications International Corporation or procured from an outside vendor, and this decision will depend principally on price. The balance of the components can be procured on a commodity basis, and do not require alliances with the suppliers. These components include the structural steel for the perimeter ring, steel pipe for the pedestal and foundation, steel pipe for the torque tubes, steel wire trusses, pipe flanges, fasteners, heliostat controller enclosure, electric power and grounding wire, and control wire.

8.5.4.2 Commercial Production Heliostats
Potential supplier alliances for the commercial production heliostats include the drives, stainless steel sheets for the membranes, and mirror coatings. An alliance with the one drive supplier starting with the early production heliostats is valuable for four reasons. First, the tooling costs can be amortized in the first production runs, which allows the cost targets for the drives to be reached with cumulative production volumes as small as possible. Second, the drives can be supplied with minimum costs for tooling amortization, overhead, and profit because the supplier is not subjected to the bidding process on each successive plant. Third, economies of scale in production runs should provide lower overhead costs and profits on each drive. Fourth,

119

expensive investments in tooling which provide small, yet important, reductions in costs become feasible.

An alliance with the supplier of stainless steel sheets is valuable for two reasons. First, stainless steel strips with a thickness of 0.003 inches are currently only available in widths up to 24 inches. With material this thin, longitudinal and transverse-rolling processing are required to prevent herringbone waves and other deformities. If production volumes justify the investment, the supplier can revise the dimensions of the raw material to new values of, for example, 36 inches wide and 0.004 inches thick.

This can reduce the costs for membrane handling and welding by one-third. Second, the raw material can be supplied with minimum costs for tooling amortization, overhead, and profit because the supplier is not subjected to the bidding process on each successive plant.

An alliance with the supplier of the mirror surface coatings may be mandatory. This is likely to be a specialty application, and the number of potential suppliers may be limited to one or two.

The balance of the components can be procured on a commodity basis, and do not require alliances with the suppliers. These components include the structural steel for the perimeter ring, steel pipe for the perimeter ring supports, fasteners, heliostat controller enclosure, electric power and grounding wire, and control wire.

8.6   Competition

The domestic and international heliostat manufacturers in competition with Science Applications International Corporation, the competitive advantage offered by the early and commercial stretched membrane designs, and the barriers to entry in the heliostat market are described below.

8.6.1   Heliostat Manufacturers

A description of the domestic and international heliostat manufacturers, and the products available or could be offered by each supplier, is outlined in the following sections.

8.6.1.1 Domestic Manufacturers

The current domestic heliostat manufacturers active in the development of central receiver projects include the following:

- Science Applications International Corporation, offering the following: a 150 m^2 stretched membrane heliostat using one reflector; a 100 m^2 stretched membrane heliostat using two 50 m^2 reflectors; and a 170m^2 stretched membrane heliostat using 22 3.2-meter diameter mirror modules. To date, the following heliostats have been installed at the National Solar Thermal Test Facility in Albuquerque, New Mexico: two 50 m^2 stretched membrane heliostats using one reflector, one 100 m^2 stretched membrane heliostat using two 50 m^2 reflectors, and one 170 m^2 multi-faceted heliostat. Three more 170 m^2 heliostats have been installed at Golden, CO, and at the Solar 2 plant. In addition, one 90 m^2 stretched membrane parabolic dish tracker, using 16 6.64 m^2 modules, has been installed at a SAIC test site in Golden, Colorado, and 120 m^2 dishes have been installed and operated at Golden, CO and in Washington, D.C.

- Solar Kinetics Incorporated, offering a 150 m^2 stretched membrane heliostat using one reflector, and a 148 m^2 glass/metal heliostat using 20 7.43 m^2 laminated glass mirror modules. To date, two 50 m^2 stretched membrane heliostats using one reflector each have been installed at the National Solar Thermal Test Facility in Albuquerque, New Mexico.

- Advanced Thermal Systems, offering the following glass/metal heliostats designs under license from ARCO Solar Incorporated: a 95.1 m^2 heliostat using 16 5.95 m^2 laminated glass mirror modules, and a 148.6 m^2 heliostat using 20 7.43 m^2 laminated glass mirror modules. To date, the following heliostats have been installed: 30 52.8 m^2 glass/metal heliostats at the 1 MW$_t$ enhanced oil recovery site in Taft, California; 106 95.1 m^2 trackers (heliostats with photovoltaic panels replacing the mirror modules) at the 1 MW$_e$ photovoltaic power plant in Hesperia, California; 750 95.1 m^2 photovoltaic trackers in the first phase of the 8 MW$_e$ photovoltaic power plant at Carrisa Plains, California; and 60 148.6 m^2 photovoltaic trackers in the second phase of the photovoltaic power plant at Carrisa Plains, California.

In addition, there are at least two manufacturers who are not currently involved in central receiver development, but could produce heliostats if the market demand warranted. The manufacturers include the following:

- Solar Power Engineering Company, offering a glass/metal heliostat with a reflector area of 200.67 m^2. The reflector uses 30 2.79 m^2 (6 feet by 5 feet) laminated glass modules. To date, one development heliostat has been installed at the National Solar Thermal Test Facility in Albuquerque, New Mexico. The selected area of 200 m^2 was based on previous evolutions in heliostat design, in which the reflector area was increased to reduce the unit weight (lb$_m$/m^2) of the structure and drive, and therefore the unit cost ($/m^2). However, a reduction in unit weight may not be possible with a structure this large if the stiffness required to retain the pointing accuracy in the outermost modules is maintained. As a result, the cost benefits for heliostats approaching an area of 200 m^2 are likely very small.

- McDonnell-Douglas Astronautics Corporation (now Boeing Corp.), offering glass/metal heliostats with reflector areas of 56.85 m^2 and nominally 100 m^2. The smaller heliostat is from the "second-generation" design program sponsored by the Department of Energy and uses 14 4.06 m^2 laminated glass modules. Several test heliostats were built, but none are currently in operation. The larger heliostat does not exist, but (presumably) could be developed from the 91 m^2 parabolic dishes fabricated for the Stirling engine demonstration projects. Several of these dishes were fabricated and tested at various sites around the country, but none are presently in operation.

8.6.1.2 International Manufactures
The current international heliostat manufacturers active in the development of central receiver projects include the following:

121

- Schlaich, Bergermann und Partner (Germany), offering a 150 m^2 stretched membrane heliostat using one module. The reflector uses 372 glass mirror segments, each 0.9 mm thick, glued to the stretched membrane. The membrane is fabricated from stainless steel strips, each 0.4 mm thick and I meter wide, and the perimeter ring is fabricated from a carbon steel channel 750 mm deep. The heliostat foundation is a circular concrete grade beam, with a diameter equal to the diameter of the reflector. The reflector is supported at the perimeter centerline by steel legs with wheels; tracking in the azimuth direction is performed with a 0.47 kW, motor driving the wheels along the circular foundation. A circular elevation ring, with a diameter equal to the diameter of the reflector, is mounted perpendicular to the reflector; tracking in the elevation direction is performed with a 0.47 kW, motor driving the ring. To date, one test heliostat has been installed at the Plataforma Solar de Ahneria in Spain.

- Asoclacion de Investigacion Industrial Eloctrica (Spain) offering the following glass/metal heliostats: a 65 m^2 heliostat using 20 3.25 m^2 mirror modules, and a 105.6 m^2 heliostat using 32 3.3 m (1.5 meters by 2.2 meters) mirror modules. In the former design, the mirrors are a laminate of 2.2 mm and 2.4 mm thick glass, bonded to an embossed steel frame. In the later design, the mirrors are 4 mm thick low-iron float glass with 3 lacquer coatings on the back for weather protection.

- Centro de Investigaciones Energoticas, Medioainblentales y Tecnologicas (Spain) offers two glass/metal heliostats. The first, GMI OOA, has a total reflector area of 105 m^2, consisting of thirty-two 3.3 m^2 rectangular mirror facets. Each facet consists of two 1.5 meters by 1.1 meters mirrors, mounted to and curved by a galvanized metal frame. The second, GMIOOB, has a total reflector area of 99 m^2, consisting of twelve 8.25 m^2 rectangular mirror facets. Each facet consists of five 1.5 meters by 1.1 meters mirrors, mounted to and curved by a profiled metal frame. Both facet types have a focal length of 480 meters.

The facets are mounted on three (GMIOOA) or two (GMIOOB) trusses, each 8 meters long, to form one of two mirror panels. The two panels are mounted on a torque tube, which are 12 meters long and 0.4 meters in diameter. The entire reflector assembly is bolted on a combination elevation-azimuth drive unit with reduction ratios on each axis of 17,820: 1. The drive is located on top of a pedestal, which is 5 meters high and 0.61 meters in diameter. Each drive motor is rated at 0.37 kW$_e$.

8.6.1.3 Near-Term Competitors
The strongest competitors in the manufacture of glass/metal and stretched membrane heliostats are discussed below.

8.6.1.3.1 Glassl/Metal Heliostats: Advanced Thermal Systems
Of the designs currently available, the 95.1 m^2 and 148.6 m^2 glass/metal heliostats from Advanced Thermal Systems are the most mature, and represent the strongest competition for the next central receiver project. Advanced Thermal Systems could respond immediately to a purchase order for several thousand heliostats, subject only to the manufacturing lead time on the drives and glass sheets for the mirror modules.

(Solmat3.to1)

Discussions with representatives from ARCO Solar Incorporated and Advanced Thermal Systems indicate that the designs are close to the theoretical optimum. The total heliostat and tracker area privately financed and installed at Hesperia and Carrisa Plains exceeds the total heliostat area installed by Martin Marietta Corporation at the 10 MW_e Solar One central receiver pilot plant. The experience gained in these installations has driven cost reduction efforts, which has produced structures with minimum unit weight, minimum field assembly labor, and competitive component sources for the glass, drives, and trusses.

Component and system reliability has also been excellent. The 106 trackers at Hesperia, which operated daily from 1983 to 1992, have been disassembled and moved to the Daggett, California, for reuse in the Solar Two project. In addition, 3,500 mirror modules from the Carrisa Plains facility have been moved to the Solar Two project site to provide the 1,696 mirrors required to convert the 106 trackers to heliostats, and to replace 1,800 mirrors lost from the Martin Marietta heliostats due to corrosion and earthquake damage. The mirror modules from Carrisa Plains have been exposed to the weather for 10 years and show numerous small cracks. However, corrosion of the silver is minimal and the degradation in reflectivity is less than 2 percentage points from the values obtained with new mirrors in 1985.

Estimating a price for the Advanced Thermal Systems heliostat is difficult task. The price is strongly dependent on the number of heliostats purchased, the cost of the drive, and the cost of the glass sheets in the mirror modules. For example, the price of a drive for a 148 m^2 heliostat can range from \$5,000 (\$34/m^2) to \$9,000 (\$61/m^2) depending on the manufacturer and scheduled delivery commitments. However, the items in the balance of the heliostat such as the torque tubes, pedestals, and trusses. are basically commodities; as such, these prices are essentially independent of the number of heliostats purchased and are as low as commercially possible. The anticipated range in prices for several heliostat purchase quantities are shown in **Table 8-9.**

If a steady commercial production rate of 5,000 heliostats per year could be established, the estimated price should decrease to a minimum value of \$120/m^2 to \$135/m^2.

Table 8-9. Estimated Installed Heliostat Prices
148.6 m^2 Glass/Metal Heliostat from Advanced Thermal Systems

Number of Heliostats Purchased	Unit Price Range, \$/m^2
100	250 – 350
1,000	175 – 200
4,000	150 – 175

8.6.1.3.2. Stretched Membrane Heliostats:
The two manufacturers competing with Science Applications International Corporation in the stretched membrane heliostat market are Solar Kinetics Incorporated and Schlaich, Bergermann

123

und Partner. Of the two, Solar Kinetics Incorporated offers the strongest near-term competition in the United States.

8.6.2 Competitive Advantage
The competitive advantages of the first commercial and fully commercial stretched membrane heliostats from Science Applications International Corporation are discussed below.

8.6.2.1 Early Commercial Plants
On the first commercial plants, the 148.6 m^2 glass/metal heliostat from Advanced Thermal Systems will be a direct competitor to the 146.2 m^2 stretched membrane heliostat. The glass/metal heliostat offers proven components, predicable optical performance, and in all probability, a competitive price.

The stretched membrane heliostat is similar in concept to the glass/metal design. The foundation, pedestal, drive, and support structure are nearly identical, and promise comparable performance. However, the optical performance and lifetime of the mirror modules are something of an unknown. If the stretched membrane design is to win a competitive procurement, the installed price of the heliostat must be at least 5 percent, and perhaps 10 percent, lower. The required selling price of the stretched membrane modules to meet these cost targets for two cases of glass/metal heliostat prices is presented in **Table 8-10.** The price of the glass mirror modules in a heliostat priced at $175/m^2 is estimated to be $70/m^2, and the price of the mirror modules in a heliostat priced at $135/m^2 is estimated to be $60/m^2.

**Table 8-10. Required Selling Prices of 2.9 Meter Diameter
Stretched Membrane Mirror Modules**

Glass/Metal Heliostat Price, $/m^2	Required Cost Advantage of Stretched Membrane Heliostat, Percent	Required Module Selling Price, $ ($/m^2)
175	5	410 (61)
175	10	350 (52)
135	5	350 (53)
135	10	310 (46)

The estimated weight of a 2.9 meter diameter stretched membrane module is 238 pounds, of which 192 pounds is structural steel, 19 pounds is stainless steel, and 27 pounds is glass. Assuming unit prices of $0.75/lb$_m$ for the fabricated perimeter ring, $3.00/lb$_m$ for the stainless steel, $40/m^2 for the glass mirror tiles (in small quantities from a sole-source vendor), $1 0/m^2 for the mirror release adhesive, and $5/m^2 for amortized tooling costs, the allowable labor contribution for each module ranges from -$250 to $150. Therefore, the present approach to the module design must evolve to be a competitive option.

124

The largest contribution to the materials price is the combination of mirror tiles and adhesive. Two approaches are possible for reducing this price. The first approach is the purchase of mirror tiles on a competitive basis and the replacement of the release adhesive with an adhesive applied by spray. If the mirror tiles can be purchased for $20/m^2$, and if the adhesive can be applied for $3/m^2$ the allowable labor contribution ranges from -$90 to $ 10.

The second approach is the replacement of the glass-silver mirrors with first-surface silver mirrors protected with a transparent aluminum oxide or carbon coating. The projected cost of the coated mirror is $10/m^2$. In addition, an adhesive is not required because the mirror is applied directly to the membrane. Under these conditions, the allowable labor contribution for each module ranges from $10 to $110. Assuming a labor rate of $20/hour, the maximum labor contribution is approximately 5 hours. For fully automated production, this labor requirement should be achievable.

In summary, if the heliostat price for the first commercial project is approximately $175/m^2$ and if an application process for the first-surface silver mirror can be successfully completed, the proposed stretched membrane design should be able to successfully compete with glass/metal heliostats. However, if allowable heliostat prices are less than $175/m^2$, two conditions must be met for stretched membrane heliostats to be a competitive option. First, designs with fewer and larger facets will need to be pursued to reduce the unit material (lb_m/m^2) requirements. Second, a commercial market for heliostats must be approaching maturity to warrant the investment in mobile tooling required for large modules.

8.6.2.2 Commercial Projects

On the fully commercial projects, a stretched membrane heliostat with a single reflector is the only concept, which can meet the cost requirements of $90/m^2$ or less. It is anticipated that design, fabrication, and reflector lifetime issues will have been resolved through research programs and small demonstration installations. Stretched membrane designs from competing suppliers will offer the same reliability, life, and optical quality as glass/metal designs, and the selection of a heliostat manufacturer will be based principally on price.

A competitive advantage for the heliostat from Science Applications International Corporation must be derived from some or all of the following effects:

- Alliances with the suppliers of the drives, who can offer a favorable price in exchange for a guaranteed supply contract.

- Advanced reflector surfaces, which offer an abrasion resistant front surface and a corrosion lifetime for the silver reflector of at least 30 years. The transparent aluminum oxide and carbon mirror coatings discussed in Section V, Manufacturing Strategy, have been the subject of some research at Science Applications International Corporation for the past several years. However, the surface properties described in Section V are based on small experimental samples, and alternate deposition procedures may need to be developed to meet the needs of commercial reflectors. If a private research program at Science Applications International Corporation can produce a ceramic or organic mirror coating which is resistant to abrasion in advance of the competition, this will offer a significant pricing advantage.

(Solmat3.to1)

- Module fabrication tooling which can be moved inexpensively from site to site.

- Alliances with the suppliers of stainless steel sheets in widths greater than 24 inches. Increasing the width of the sheets will reduce the cost of welding the membrane, and improve the optical quality of the finished reflector by reducing the number of seams.

8.6.3 Barriers to Entry
There are few barriers to entry in the manufacture and installation of glass/metal heliostats. Although the design from Advanced Thermal Systems is licensed from ARCO Solar Incorporated, there should be little difficulty in producing a similar design that did not infringe on the protected features. Possible approaches to a similar or comparable design might include the following:

Drives
Azimuth and elevation drives for heliostats from various manufacturers, with nominal reflector areas of 100 m^2 to 150 m^2, have already been developed under Department of Energy and private funding by Flenders, Peerless-Winsmith, and Hub City. Any or all of these manufacturers could readily produce a drive in response to a performance specification.

Mirror Modules
The mirror modules on the Advanced Thermal Systems heliostat consist of a 1 mm thick low-iron glass mirror laminated to a 3 mm thick glass sheet, to which is glued sheet metal hat sections to support and curve the glass laminate. The proprietary feature is the sheet metal supports; the laminated mirrors are available on a commercial basis. Alternate, and equally effective, supports should be easy to develop, and the production of a reliable mirror module should be a straightforward exercise.

Support Structure
The support structure consists of the following: a spiral wound steel pipe, which forms the combination foundation and pedestal; two pipe sections, which form the torque tubes; four steel bar joists, which support the mirror modules; and a collection of pipe flanges. All of these components are standard, commercial structural steel shapes.

Heliostat Controller
The heliostat controller is a small microprocessor that interprets commands from a central computer, and controls the motion of the azimuth and elevation drive motors to point the heliostat in the correct direction. The performance requirements are relatively basic, and several heliostat manufacturers have independently produced functional controllers.

Heliostat Array Controller Software
The array controller software responds to plant operating mode commands, periodically computes the sun position, and periodically calculates the new pointing vector for each heliostat The effort required to develop the code would not be minimal; however, several heliostat manufacturers have independently produced functional programs.

(Solmat3.to1)

The barriers to entry in the manufacture and installation of stretched membrane heliostats are more formidable. The comments above regarding the duplication of the support structure, heliostat controller, and heliostat array controller software apply to both the glass/metal heliostat and the stretched membrane heliostat. However, the fabrication of the reflectors and the approach to the focus control system for the stretched membrane heliostats involve considerable fabrication experience and proprietary designs, respectively.

For example, there are several steps in the fabrication of a mirror module that can only be perfected through the experience gained by trial-and-error. These include: resistance welding 5 to 13 m^2 metal foil strips, each 2 feet wide, side-by-side without forming small-scale dips or large-scale waves; handling thin metal sheets up to 26 feet in diameter; forming perimeter rings 10 to 26 feet in diameter, with out-of-plane dimensions less than 0.1 percent of the diameter; isotropically tensioning the membranes to 10,000 lb_f/m^2 to 20,000 lb_f/m^2 (depending on the material) prior to resistance welding the edges to the perimeter rings; and resistance welding a stainless steel sheet 0.003 inches thick to a carbon steel perimeter ring (or an aluminum sheet 0.010 inches thick to an aluminum perimeter ring), yet insuring a corrosion lifetime of at least 30 years.

Two effective, and proprietary, reflector focus control systems have been developed to date. Science Applications International Corporation uses a gear actuator to move the rear membrane. Pushing the rear membrane forward increases the pressure in the inter-membrane plenum, and thereby increases the radius of curvature of the front membrane. Similarly, pulling the rear membrane back decreases the radius of curvature of the front membrane. A linear variable differential transducer connected to the front membrane provides a feedback signal to the focus control system. Solar Kinetics Incorporated uses a variable speed, reversing axial fan to evacuate or pressurize the inter-membrane plenum, and a linear variable differential transducer to monitor the position of the front membrane. Alternate focus control systems can undoubtedly be developed; however, field tests of prototype systems will be required to ensure that response times are adequate on windy days.

Although both Science Applications International Corporation and Solar Kinetics Incorporated have considerable experience in stretched membrane heliostat technology, neither company has fabricated a commercial-size heliostat using one 150 m^2 reflector. To date, only one such heliostat has been installed, and this is a test installation at the Plataforma Solar de Almeria by Schlaich, Bergermann und Partner.

8.7   Technical and Management Experience

As outlined in Section 8.2, Business Strategy, the responsibility for the design, fabrication, installation, warranty, and guarantee of the collector system will be distributed among several companies. The technical and management experience of potential contractors and component suppliers is described below.

8.7.1 Items Provided by Science Applications International Corporation

Science Applications International Corporation (SAIC) has fabricated four prototype 50 m^2 stretched membrane modules, fabricated over 100 modules in the range of 3 m^2 to 5 m^2, installed three demonstration heliostats at the National Solar Thermal Test Facility in Albuquerque, New Mexico, and installed two demonstration parabolic dish concentrators at the SAIC test site in Golden, Colorado. These activities have developed the resident experience to provide the following:

- Heliostat structural analysis. Unit prices for commercial heliostats ($/$m^2$) will be determined almost exclusively by the unit weight (lb_m/m^2). To reduce the unit weight as far as possible, one company must be responsible for the overall analysis of the entire heliostat using a finite element computer code.

- Stretched membrane mirror modules, based on the proprietary experience necessary for membrane strip welding, perimeter ring fabrication, membrane-to-ring resistance welding, and application of reflective surfaces.

- Software for the heliostat controller and the heliostat array controller. The software should be developed by one company to ensure reliable communications, and to incorporate the unique requirements of reflector focusing, automatic defocusing, or (perhaps) active canting.

8.7.2 Items Provided by Other Contractors

Outside contractors are best suited to provide the balance of the heliostat components and the collector system, as follows:

- Regarding the collector and receiver system optimization, the sophisticated computer codes, such as R-CELL in the United States and HFLCAL in Europe, optimize the radial and azimuthal heliostat locations, tower height, and receiver dimensions to provide the lowest levelized cost of thermal energy from the receiver. The receiver dimensions are selected in conjunction with the receiver supplier to satisfy the constraints of peak flux as a function of bulk nitrate salt temperature. In general, the codes have not been developed for public use, and operation and interpretation remain something of an art. Most of the experience in the use of R-CELL resides with the University of Houston, and in the use of HFLCAL with Interatom GmbH and Deutsche Forschungsanstalt fur Luft- und Raumfahrt e.V. in Germany.

- Flenders, Peerless-Winsmith, Hub City, Allen-Bradley, and Dodge are the drive companies that have the casting equipment, tooling, and experience required to produce reliable drives at a moderate price for the initial commercial projects, and at a low cost in the quasi-mass production quantities for the commercial projects.

- The Heliostat controllers are essentially a microprocessor with electric power relays, and should be less complex than a video cassette recorder. As such, assembly of the controllers should probably be performed by suppliers involved in consumer electronics.

(Solmat3.to1)

Commodity items, such as structural steel, fasteners, and bulk materials are provided by any number of steel fabricators and suppliers in industry.

(Solmat3.to1)

9.0   Lessons Learned and Phase III Planning

9.1   Phase II Lessons Learned

Phase II of the SOLMAT program has met its primary objectives of building and demonstrating key pieces of automated tooling, and successfully fielding and demonstrating four faceted stretched-membrane heliostats. Shown below are the major lessons learned on the project in terms of both what worked well, and future improvements needed.

- The semi-automated tooling that was built in Phase II has been very successful in reducing the labor cost of fabricating facets. A reduction in labor of 74% was demonstrated as compared to pre-SOLMAT methods. The tooling selected for automation was identified in Phase I to have the best cost/benefit ratio, resulting in the large impact on labor costs.

- The single production line for both dish and heliostat facets has proven effective in reducing tooling costs for both technologies.

- Inspection/quality control is a critical issue when transitioning from an R&D environment to production. Procedures must be in place to assure repeatability of fabrication processes. Manufacturing tooling must be simple to operate, and produce repeatable results. Maintenance must be performed on a regular basis. Operators must be well trained and conscious of quality control.

- An incident involving accelerated corrosion of the facets due to road salt spray deposited in shipping has pointed out the potential danger of field corrosion, specifically on weld sites where sensitization may occur. A switch from Type 201 stainless steel for the membranes and Type 409 for the rings to Type 316L for both is being considered.

- The heliostat currently uses 3/32 in glass mirror tiles, while the dish uses 1.0 mm thick glass. Using the thicker glass for heliostats has been successful in reducing the glass cost from $4.00/ft2 to $0.50/ft2.

- The first Phase II heliostat initially had a problem with excessive sag of the torque tubes due to gravity loading. The problem pointed out the need for thorough FEM structural analysis, followed up with hand calculations as a check. More accurate wind load data is also needed to provide an optimized structure.

- Controls and sensor reliability is a major issue which could significantly increase O&M costs. More work is needed to ruggedize the controls.

- Wind at the field site can have a serious installation cost and schedule impact. The installation crew had to wait two months for the wind to die down at Solar Two. A method is needed to install heliostats in a wind higher than 5 mph, which is the current limit.

(Solmat3.to1)

- SAIC's 170 m2 heliostat is best suited for larger fields, where image size and off-axis aberration are not an issue. A smaller version with fewer facets can easily be developed for smaller fields.

- A reliable, low cost drive with the required load capacity is needed to make heliostats cost effective. Current drives are in the range of $15,000 each in quantities of 50.

9.2   PHASE III PLANNING

Significant strides were made in Phase II of the project in fabrication and demonstration of tooling, and also demonstration of reduction in labor content of heliostat components. Through the development of an advanced welding and tensioning tool, and incremental improvements in other process areas, we successfully reduced the labor required to build a single stretched membrane mirror module to approximately 20 man/hours per unit. Labor prior to the Solmat II Initiative was approximately 77 man/hours per single mirror module unit.

During the mirror module manufacturing stages of the Solmat II and JVP Phase II Program, several areas within the manufacturing process were identified as needing additional improvement. These improvements would upgrade our present mirror module manufacturing capability, allowing for a more consistent and QA verifiable process, thus enhancing quality and reducing facet manufacturing labor costs. Under a modest improvement program, a two shift operation could produce facets for approximately 60 dish\Stirling systems per year. If the line was producing facets for heliostat systems, production capability would be placed at 45 systems per year due the additional number of facets needed on the present heliostat design.

An outline and cost summary of our Phase III estimate is shown on **Table 9-1**. Phase III is broken down into two sub-phases; Phase III-A engineering and tooling design, and Phase III-B tooling fabrication and testing. The main focus of Phase III is quality and repeatability improvement in the manufacturing process.

The investment needed to upgrade the present manufacturing capability would be in the form of state-of-the-art roll resistance or laser welding technology, process flow improvements, out-sourcing of certain components, QA verifiable process improvement, and general facilities and manufacturing space improvements.   Tooling designs proposed for long-range manufacturing capabilities (200+ systems per year) must incorporate this advanced welding technology, as well as, other specified tooling design requirements that have been identified through the Solmat Phase II experience, and as would be outlined in a comprehensive manufacturing plan and manufacturing design strategy. As markets forces dictate, the present planning strategy is to improve the existing equipment in conjunction with pursuing detailed design packages for an advanced 200 system per year facet manufacturing capability. We would refrain from building the actual tooling until market demands can justify the investment.

Proposed upgrades to our present capability under the Solmat Phase III Initiative should contain the following line items:

(Solmat3.to1)

- Move existing equipment to more suitable facility.
- Design and implement dedicated facet ring weldment fixture.
- Incorporate roll forming tooling to form facet ring channels.
- Incorporate state-of-the-art welding equipment into the present membrane welding and tensioning equipment.
- Design and incorporate new QA verifiable tracking mechanism into present membrane seam welding equipment.
- Improve upon membrane tensioning clip arrangement to reduce engagement and disengagement time.
- Design automated membrane trimmer\cutter attachment to trim facet after tensioning and welding process has been completed.
- Design and implement a more advanced glass application station, allowing the installation of the mirrored tiles to be accomplished directly down-stream of the facet tensioning and welding process.
- Commit the necessary resources to develop detailed manuals documenting the manufacturing, QA, maintenance and installation processes.

132

Table 9-1. SolMaT Phase III ROM Cost Estimate

SolMaT Phase III ROM Cost Estimate
Rev 4

K. Beninga 8/28/98

Phase III-A Engineering and Tooling Design   (POP11/1/98-7/1/99)

	Total	Labor	Materials
Concentrator Component Cost Reduction			
Support Structure Weight Reduction	$ 150,000	$ 150,000	
Adhesive/Edge Seal Selection/Test	$ 35,000	$ 30,000	$ 5,000
Controls reliability/user interface	$ 50,000	$ 45,000	$ 5,000
Heliostat Test Support	$ 70,000	$ 65,000	$ 5,000
Facet Materials Selection and Test	$ 50,000	$ 45,000	$ 5,000
Subtotal	$ 355,000	$ 335,000	$ 20,000
Manufacturing Development - Design			
Production Line Layout/Optimization	$ 75,000	$ 75,000	
Full Production Tooling Preliminary Design	$ 100,000	$ 100,000	
Quality Improvements - Automate ring welding	$ 20,000	$ 20,000	$ -
Ring cleaning station	$ 5,000	$ 5,000	$ -
Improved membrane welder	$ 20,000	$ 20,000	$ -
Improved membrane tension/weld	$ 40,000	$ 40,000	$ -
Improved adhesive/glass application	$ 20,000	$ 20,000	$ -
Manufacturing/Installation/QA Manuals	$ 50,000	$ 50,000	
Project Management	$ 75,000	$ 75,000	
Subtotal	$ 405,000	$ 405,000	$ -
Phase III-A Subtotal	$ 760,000	$ 740,000	$ 20,000

Phase III-B Tooling Fabrication and Testing   (POP8/1/99-8/1/00)

	Total	Labor	Materials
Manufacturing Quality Improvement - Fabrication of Tooling			
Automate ring welding	$ 25,000	$ 10,000	$ 15,000
Ring cleaning station	$ 25,000	$ 5,000	$ 20,000
Improved membrane welder	$ 30,000	$ 5,000	$ 25,000
Improved membrane tension/weld (roll resistance)	$ 100,000	$ 20,000	$ 80,000
automated adhesive/glass application	$ 50,000	$ 10,000	$ 40,000
Project Management	$ 75,000	$ 75,000	$ -
Subtotal	$ 305,000	$ 125,000	$ 180,000
Facet Production Verification			
Production Supervision	$ 30,000	$ 30,000	
Component Production (per facet)	$ 1,700	$ 600	$ 1,100
Subtotal (50 units)	$ 115,000	$ 60,000	$ 55,000
Phase III-B Subtotal	$ 420,000	$ 185,000	$ 235,000
Total Phase III Project Cost	$ 1,180,000	$ 925,000	$ 255,000
NREL Portion @ 80%	$ 944,000		
Industry Portion @ 20%	$ 236,000		

133

(Solmat3.to1)

Incident Report #	Date/ Time	Initiated by	Incident Description	Time to repair (hrs):	Relevant	Conc.	Controls
117	8/1/97 9:00:00 AM	Russell Forristall	While connecting control computer discovered that the elevation encoder was not registering.		✓	☐	✓
118	8/6/97 11:00:00 AM	Russell Forristall	Elevation encoder failed.	23.5	✓	✓	☐
121	8/8/97 8:00:00 AM	Russell Forristall	Corroded azimuth motor cable connector.	1.15	✓	✓	☐
122	8/11/97 7:00:00 AM	Russell Forristall	Installing new diagonal support rod bracket.	3.75	✓	✓	☐
123	8/13/97 11:07:00 AM	Russell Forristall	Lost power to the heliostat and controller.	0.67	✓	☐	✓
124	8/28/97 9:30:00 AM	Russell Forristall	Oil seal on the azimuth angled gear box was leaking.	5	✓	✓	☐
28	9/4/97 10:00:00 AM	Russell Forristall	Edge seal gaskets mounted on the facet rings are retaining water.		☐	☐	☐
125	9/13/97 8:00:00 AM	Russell Forristall	Communication driver controller chip failed. This chip is located in the controller box on the pedestal.	29.75	✓	☐	✓
30	9/13/97 6:15:00 PM	Roger Davenport	blown controller chips due to lightening strike	30	✓	☐	✓
126	9/15/97 4:45:00 PM	Russell Forristall	Azimuth motor was oscillating east and west.	16.25	✓	✓	☐
127	9/16/97 10:00:00 AM	Russell Forristall	Heliostat lost communication with the network and started to move to the upward stow position.	2	✓	☐	✓
128	10/29/97 1:38:00 PM	Russell Forristall	The heliostat unexpectedly began moving to a new orientation over its shoulder.	0.6	✓	☐	✓

Incident Report #	Date/ Time	Initiated by	Incident Description	Time to repair (hrs):	Relevant	Conc.	Controls
129	11/15/97 8:00:00 AM	Russell Forristall	Elevation fuse blew when trying to move the heliostat from the stow position to tracking.	0.75	☑	☑	☐
130	1/14/98 8:00:00 AM	Russell Forristall	Took the controller PC off-line so that some components could be upgraded.		☐	☐	☐
71	2/3/98 3:00:00 PM	Roger Davenport	Elevation encoder has apparent failed. One output shows around 3V and doesn't vary with motion. The other output goes from near 0V to around 4.5V, as it should. This happened while Jack Allread was hooking up his sensor inputs to monitor the heliostat position. We will replace the encoder on 2/4 and bring it to the office for evaluation.	32.22	☑	☑	☑
98	3/10/98 2:30:00 PM	Philip Cuka	Heliostat continued to track after high wind stow alarm continuously sounding. JVP 2 had already stowed, but heliostat was still tracking.	2333.5	☑	☐	☑
116	3/23/98 6:20:00 AM	Russell Forristall	PC controller computer froze up when I tried to open up AccuSet. I had to cycle power to the computer to get all the software to work properly.		☐	☐	☐
120	3/25/98 12:45:00 PM	Russell Forristall	The heliostat controller software did not respond to the high wind detection from the network box. The high wind alarm was sounding for more than 60 seconds without the high wind status triggering on the controller screen. The setting in the Host.cfg file for a high wind trigger is 30 seconds.		☐	☐	☐
132	3/27/98 8:35:00 AM	Roger Davenport	Noticed a hole in the rear membrane of a facet. (See A on attached drawing.) Water began running out with system in face-up position. Hole appears to be about 4-5 cm long, 1/2 - 1 cm wide. There appears to be some corrosion around the hole.		☐	☐	☐
134	4/1/98 11:00:00 AM	Carl Bingham	2-Heliostat Control Program: In manual move mode - Start position 180.05 +/- 0.05 "1m 180 05 89" - Azimuth motor moves 180.05 +/- 0.05 "1m 180 89" - Azimuth motor moves Also, Help screen implies nM az, el syntax, should be nM az el (no comma)		☐	☐	☐
142	4/7/98 6:15:00 AM	Russell Forristall	After arriving at the site, I put the heliostat into the tracking mode. Because the sun was below the minimum elevation, I expected the heliostat to put itself into the nightstow mode, but the heliostat started to move to the tracking position. The reason this happened was because someone adjusted the system clock to daylight savings time without adjusting the GMT in the parameter files. I adjusted the clock back and the heliostat moved back to the Nightstow position. I thought I solved the problem, but the heliostat did not wake up when the sun passed the minimum sun elevation. I had to reboot the program to get the heliostat to track.		☐	☐	☐

Incident Report #	Date/ Time	Initiated by	Incident Description	Time to repair (hrs):	Relevant	Conc.	Controls
176	4/25/98 8:00:00 AM	James Sellars	Untied the Heliostat and switched from local to auto mode at the pedestal as usual before initiating a command to track on target (1T). When I commanded the heliostat on target the heliostat goal changed to the target position (as it should) but changed back to the stow position within 2 or 3 seconds. The heliostat control screen then displayed that the motors had been disabled. I went outside to the base of the heliostat pedestal for further diagnosis. I found that the Z-World controller was behaving strangely. The LED on the control board, when in run mode, should blink once every second or so. Since this was not the case, I reset the board. The LED continued to blink several times quickly followed by a pause and more quick flashes. I tried unplugging power to the little PLC for a minute or two and then plugging it back in, but there was no change. Update: On Monday Russ was able to cut power to the PLC and reset it.	48	✓	☐	✓
173	4/30/98	Russell Forristall	Mirrors on two facets on the west side of the heliostat have extensive cracking due to loads carried through the facets. (see sketches of the cracks on the mirror survey form.		☐	☐	☐
172	4/30/98	Russell Forristall	The back stainless steel membranes on five facets are showing signs of corrosion. Three of these facets have quarter size holes as a result of the corrosion. (see photos and layout sketch)		☐	☐	☐
171	4/30/98	Russell Forristall	The threaded portion of the diagonal support rods are rusting. (see photos)		☐	☐	☐
170	4/30/98	Russell Forristall	Paint is chipping off the torque tube stiffeners. (see photos)		☐	☐	☐
169	4/30/98	Russell Forristall	Trusses are rusting along the edges and where the truss webbing connects to the bottom and top angle irons. (see photos)		☐	☐	☐
190	5/7/98 6:30:00 AM	Philip Cuka	Heliostat started tracking about 6:13am. At approximately 6:30 I noticed that the heliostat had stopped. I reset the network box, little PLC, power and computer. All these actions had no effect. I found that a 32V, 10A fuse had blown. Location: Right fuse of two-fuse set to left of AZ and EL relays in pedestal box. Talked with Roger who indicated that the fuse should be 110V, 20A ceramic. Found and installed a 250V 20A fuse. Commanded heliostat to track, and it is now working.	2	✓	✓	☐
203	5/26/98 6:00:00 AM	Philip Cuka	Static/buzzing sound coming from Little PLC. Little PLC light did not come on when P1 cable plugged in. HELIOSTAT COMMUNICATION FAILURE message appeared when system commanded to track.	360	✓	☐	✓

Incident Report #	Date/ Time	Initiated by	Incident Description	Time to repair (hrs):	Relevant	Conc.	Controls
240	6/18/98 6:40:00 AM	Russell Forristall	System would not move due to an elevation motor fault.	3	☑	☑	☐
251	8/3/98	Roger Davenport	Heliostat and network board do not respond Mark Mehos and Jim Sellars tried various things to reprogram/troubleshoot, but no success. There were several lightning strikes over the weekend prior to this. The heliostat had been operating prior to that time.		☐	☐	☐
260	9/14/98	Roger Davenport	9/14: Encoder E004 failed and removed from Elevation. Tested: 27 ma near was OK, 4.8/0 near was OK, 1.0/0 far was Bad.		☐	☐	☐
			9/16: Encoder E005 failed and removed from Azimuth. Tested: 27 ma was OK, 4.9/0 near was OK, 1.4/0 far was Bad.				

Reliability Data

		System	Conc.	Controls
Total # of Incidents =	32			
Relevant Incidents		18	9	9
Total Hours of Operation as of	6/25/98	1263.44	1075.4	1263.44
Mean Time-Between-Failures (MTBF) hrs		64.5	119	140
Mean Time-to-Repair (MTTR) hrs		165	9.74	320
Probability of failure-free operation, for a time period, $t = 8$ hrs		88%	94%	94%

REPORT DOCUMENTATION PAGE

Form Approved
OMB NO. 0704-0188

Public reporting burden for this collection of information is estimated to average 1 hour per response, including the time for reviewing instructions, searching existing data sources, gathering and maintaining the data needed, and completing and reviewing the collection of information. Send comments regarding this burden estimate or any other aspect of this collection of information, including suggestions for reducing this burden, to Washington Headquarters Services, Directorate for Information Operations and Reports, 1215 Jefferson Davis Highway, Suite 1204, Arlington, VA 22202-4302, and to the Office of Management and Budget, Paperwork Reduction Project (0704-0188), Washington, DC 20503.

1. AGENCY USE ONLY (Leave blank)	2. REPORT DATE	3. REPORT TYPE AND DATES COVERED
	September 1998	Subcontractor report

4. TITLE AND SUBTITLE	5. FUNDING NUMBERS
HELIOSTAT MANUFACTURING FOR NEAR-TERM MARKETS, PHASE II FINAL REPORT	Task #: SE416061, SE517060, SE617043, SE717006

6. AUTHOR(S)
Science Applications International Corporation

7. PERFORMING ORGANIZATION NAME(S) AND ADDRESS(ES)	8. PERFORMING ORGANIZATION REPORT NUMBER
Science Applications International Corporation 15374 W. 6th Avenue Golden, CO 80401	

9. SPONSORING/MONITORING AGENCY NAME(S) AND ADDRESS(ES)	10. SPONSORING/MONITORING AGENCY REPORT NUMBER
National Renewable Energy Laboratory 1617 Cole Boulevard Golden, CO 80401-3393	NREL/SR-550-25837

11. SUPPLEMENTARY NOTES

12a. DISTRIBUTION/AVAILABILITY STATEMENT	12b. DISTRIBUTION CODE
National Technical Information Service U.S. Department of Commerce 5285 Port Royal Road Springfield, VA 22161	UC-600

13. ABSTRACT *(Maximum 200 words)* This report describes a project by Science Applications International Corporation and its subcontractors Boeing/Rocketdyne and Bechtel Corp. to develop manufacturing technology for production of SAIC stretched membrane heliostats. The project consists of three phases, of which two are complete. This first phase as its goals to identify and complete a detailed evaluation of manufacturing technology, process changes, and design enhancements to be pursued for near-term heliostat markets. In the second phase, the design of the SAIC stretched membrane heliostat was refined, manufacturing tooling for mirror facet and structural component fabrication was implemented, and four proof-of-concept/test heliostats were produced and installed in three locations. The proposed plan for Phase III calls for improvements in production tooling to enhance product quality and prepare increased production capacity. This project is part of the U.S. Department of Energy's Solar Manufacturing Technology Program (SolMaT).

14. SUBJECT TERMS power towers, central receivers, heliostats, reflectors, solar power, concentrating solar power, csp, mirrors, SAIC, SolMaT	15. NUMBER OF PAGES 144
	16. PRICE CODE

17. SECURITY CLASSIFICATION OF REPORT	18. SECURITY CLASSIFICATION OF THIS PAGE	19. SECURITY CLASSIFICATION OF ABSTRACT	20. LIMITATION OF ABSTRACT

NSN 7540-01-280-5500

Standard Form 298 (Rev. 2-89)
Prescribed by ANSI Std. Z39-18
298-102

CPSIA information can be obtained at www.ICGtesting.com
Printed in the USA
BVOW02s0956051114

373810BV00016B/221/P